Overcoming America's Unfair Housing Acts

OVERCOMING AMERICA'S UNFAIR HOUSING ACTS

Marcia Johnson

Overcoming America's Unfair Housing Acts

Marcia Johnson

Published by:

Vandeplas Publishing, LLC – August 2022

801 International Parkway, 5th Floor
Lake Mary, FL. 32746
USA

www.vandeplaspublishing.com

ISBN 978-1-60042-541-7

Acknowledgments

There are so many people who have provided counsel and solace over the many years I committed to service. My focus has been principally service to the African American community of which I am a life-long member, but my interest covers a much broader landscape. It has been important to serve, where I could, the disenfranchised, downtrodden, silenced, abused, hungry, unsheltered members of the human race. It has been distinctively my pleasure to work with so many people who have shared these ideals, who have helped me develop my own goals and voice and who have loved, laughed, cried, reflected, sworn, learned and taught with me over the years.

I want to more specifically acknowledge the hard work and efforts of some young lawyers who helped research this book, **Abraham Hernandez, Adetinuke Thomas**, and **Arionne Wells**. I specially thank and acknowledge **L. Anthony Johnson** for his research, writing, editing and critiquing of the book throughout the process. I also thank **Andreience Fields** for her administrative assistance.

Dedication

I dedicate this book to my family

CONTENTS

OVERCOMING AMERICA'S UNFAIR HOUSING ACTS

Introduction

It is indisputable that America has a long history of race, gender, nationality and ethnicity discrimination. From the landing on American shores, discrimination has served as a guiding principle for American social, judicial, economic policies and practices. Among other things, discriminatory policies have undergirded voting practices, education access and attainment, policing, personal welfare, access to opportunity in contracting, and property ownership.[1] Property ownership has had a significant impact on social and economic well-being. Historically, the right to vote and access to education were reserved to property owners, making them a preferred class of Americans to the detriment of those who did not own property.[2] Property ownership continues to portend opportunity, wealth, and success, and is therefore a major factor in individual and societal growth and development. To have denied people the opportunity to own and retain property constituted a general denial of health, wealth, and welfare seen to this day.

In this book, I explore this phenomenon of denial of equal rights and access as a fundamental element in creating and maintaining an American class system identifiable in large part by race and ethnicity. Not all property ownership is equal and for purposes of this book we restrict our examination to home

1 Danyelle Solomon, Connor Maxwell, and Abril Castro, Systematic Inequality and American Democracy, Center for American Progress, August 7, 2019. retrieved from https://www.americanprogress.org/issues/race/reports/2019/08/07/473003/systematic-inequality-american-democracy/ and See; Linda Darling-Hammond, Unequal Opportunity: Race and Education, Brookings Institute, March 1, 1998. retrieved from https://www.brookings.edu/articles/unequal-opportunity-race-and-education/

2 Washington State Office of the Secretary of State. retrieved from https://www.sos.wa.gov/_assets/elections/history-of-voting-in-america-timeline.pdf Also see; Barry M. Bloom, Property Ownership Versus the Right to Vote: A Question of Equal Protection, SMU Law Review, Vol 25 Issue 4 Article 8, 1971, retrieved from https://scholar.smu.edu/cgi/viewcontent.cgi?article=3381&context=smulr

LaToya Baldwin Clark, Education as Property, Virginia Law Review Association, Vol 105, retrieved from https://www.virginialawreview.org/sites/virginialawreview.org/files/BaldwinClark_Book.pdf

ownership, because it is generally accepted as the single most important basis for wealth in America.[3]

I also attempt to provide some perspective about why racial segregation continues to this day and suggest that its roots lie in institutionalized racism which is so ingrained in everything that we do that it creates barriers incredibly difficult to escape. It is important to note that while the focus of this book is the creation, maintenance and impact of housing discrimination on African Americans, to varying degrees, discriminatory practices have targeted other people of color and poor whites throughout our nation's history.

Institutionalized slavery and pervasive myths of inferiority

The promise of equality declared in 1776 did not apply to all Americans; noticeably women, Native Americans and African Americans. From America's first pronouncement of the promise to recognize certain truths, specifically the equality of men and the inalienability of certain rights, the promise proved vacuous.[4] The declaration was not intended to include all men, literally or metaphorically.[5] Instead, it took the American Civil War, several constitutional amendments, multiple Supreme Court rulings, and various Congressional acts before women, Native Americans and African Americans were able to exercise basal rights as American citizens.[6] Rights which to this day continue to be denied.

---

3 Erin Currier & Sheida Elmi, The Racial Wealth Gap and Today's American Dream, The Pew Charitable Trusts, February 16, 2018 stating [that] "homeownership [is]—a main driver of wealth—in the United States: According to the U.S. Census Bureau, the white homeownership rate as of the fourth quarter of 2017 was 72.7 percent, while the black homeownership rate was 42.1 percent—the largest such disparity since World War II." retrieved from https://www.pewtrusts.org/en/research-and-analysis/articles/2018/02/16/the-racial-wealth-gap-and-todays-american-dream

4 The Declaration of Independence states: *We hold these truths to be self-evident, that all men are created equal, that they are endowed by their Creator with certain unalienable Rights that among these are Life, Liberty and the pursuit of Happiness."*

5 Thomas Jefferson: Liberty & Slavery. The Jefferson Monticello. Retrieved from https://www.monticello.org/slavery-at-monticello/liberty-slavery

6 African Americans were declared United States citizens by the 14th Amendment to the United States Constitution, and African American men were given the right to vote by the 15th amendment to the United States Constitution. Women received the right to vote in 1920, when the 19th Amendment to the Constitution was finally ratified.

The Indian Citizens Act of 1924 conferred citizenship to Native Americans who would not get the right to vote until 1962, when Utah became the last state to confer such rights. See generally, Becky Little, Native Americans Weren't Guaranteed the Right to Vote in every state until 1962, November 6, 2018, updated Nov

Slavery was so crucial to the burgeoning nation that it was protected by its institutionalization in the Constitution of the United States. Article IV, section 2, clause 3 contains the Fugitive Slave Clause, which provides;

> *"No person held to service or labour in one state, under the laws thereof, escaping into another, shall, in consequence of any law or regulation therein, be discharged from such service or labour, but shall be delivered up on claim of the party to whom such service or labour may be due."*

In 1793, Congress went further and enacted the Fugitive Slave Act in order to give greater effect to the Fugitive Slave Clause. After passage of the Fugitive Slave Act, refugee slaves were at risk for recapture and children of fugitive slave mothers were classified as property of the mother's owner for their whole lives.

The slave-master relationship and the overall institution of slavery set up the groundwork for the centuries of inequality African Americans continue to endure. As an institution, slavery is inherently unequal. The slave system deemed the master superior to the slave and served as the basis for many long standing racist stereotypes that dehumanized African Americans. The dehumanization allowed many white Americans to justify their unrelentingly truculent treatment of African Americans by, among other things, categorizing slaves as chattel.[7]

Slavery was abolished with the ratification of the Thirteenth Amendment on December 6, in 1865,[8] more than 300 years after the first officially recognized slave ship docked on American shores.[9] These three hundred plus six years created and sowed the fertile ground for the growth, development, and institutionalism of racism throughout American society. Racism became so deeply embedded that many later efforts to right the wrongs would fail because the efforts themselves were rooted in racist stereotypes and untruths.

The ratification of the Thirteenth Amendment to the United States Constitution, for example, was written to formally abolish slavery making it

---

13 2020; retrieved from https://www.history.com/news/native-american-voting-rights-citizenship

7 Darlene Goring, The History of Slave Marriage in the United States, Louisiana State University Law Center, 2006. retrieved from https://digitalcommons.law.lsu.edu/cgi/viewcontent.cgi?referer=&httpsredir=1&article=1262&context=faculty_scholarship

8 *U.S. Constitution.* Amend. XIII

9 Crystal Ponti, America's History of Slavery Began Long Before Jamestown, History Stories, August 26, 2019 retrieved from https://www.history.com/news/american-slavery-before-jamestown-1619

unconstitutional. Yet northern and southern states were quick to circumvent the language and intent of the 13th, 14th, and 15th amendments by enacting state laws that targeted African Americans in order to limit their exercise of the newly gained rights. Commonly known as Black Codes, these laws were enacted to limit African Americans' access to equality under the law. The United States Supreme Court's *Plessy v. Ferguson* ruling cemented the nation's reliance on racial inequality when the Court adopted the separate but equal doctrine,[10] and therein kick-started segregation in public facilities on a national scale.[11]

Plessy challenged the Louisiana's Separate Car Act. The statute required "equal, but separate" railway car accommodations and legally forced Blacks into separate cars.[12] Homer Adolph Plessy was a Louisiana resident of mixed descent, having one-eighth African and seven-eighths Caucasian ancestry, who sat in one of the railway cars designated for whites. He was arrested after he refused to move to a railway car designated for Blacks. Plessy challenged the statute as a violation of the Thirteenth and Fourteenth Amendments.[13]

The Supreme Court ruled against Plessy and declared that the statute was within constitutional limitations. Among other things, the court rejected Plessy's claim that the separation of the races created a state-sanctioned badge of inferiority. The Supreme Court reasoned that while the Fourteenth Amendment's *goal* was equality, it was not intended to eliminate every distinction such as race. The court's ruling served to justify racial discrimination under the theory of *social equality* which relates to how people treat and perceive each other,

---

10 Plessy, 163 U.S. 537 at 551 (1896). The Supreme Court holding the Louisiana statute constitutional stating, "So far, then, as a conflict with the Fourteenth Amendment is concerned, the case reduces itself to the question whether the statute of Louisiana is a reasonable regulation, and with respect to this there must necessarily be a large discretion on the part of the legislature. In determining the question of reasonableness it is at liberty to act with reference to the established usages, customs and traditions of the people, and with a view to the promotion of their comfort, and the preservation of the public peace and good order. Gauged by this standard, we cannot say that a law which authorizes or even requires the separation of the two races in public conveyances is unreasonable, or more obnoxious to the Fourteenth Amendment than the acts of Congress requiring separate schools for colored children in the District of Columbia, the constitutionality of which does not seem to have been questioned, or the corresponding acts of state legislatures."

11 Abraham L. Davis & Barbara Luck Graham, The Supreme Court, Race And Civil Rights 17-28 (1995).

12 Supra Note 10 at 551-52.

13 Supra Note 10 at 442. ("The constitutionality of this act is attacked upon the ground that it conflicts both with the Thirteenth Amendment of the Constitution, abolishing slavery, and the Fourteenth Amendment, which prohibits certain restrictive legislation on the part of the States.")

distinguishing it from *political equality*, which relates to equal treatment under the law.[14] The effect was that so long as people were treated equally under the law, how people were treated and perceived socially was not actionable.

Plessy's "separate but equal" precept enhanced the spread of segregation from 1896 until 1954, when the doctrine fell in *Brown v. Board of Education.*[15] In *Brown*, the Supreme Court held that "separate but equal" facilities were inherently unequal and violated the Equal Protection Clause of the Fourteenth Amendment.[16] Brown specifically dealt with segregation in education,[17] and it would take several more Supreme Court rulings lasting well into the 1970s before segregation as a mandate was removed from all laws, including housing laws.[18] Thus, from 1896 to well with into the 20th century, government and judicially sanctioned segregation persisted.[19]

With state-imposed segregation having been upheld as constitutional and as a valid use of the states' police powers, various other methods intended to further segregation arose resulting in severe limitations on housing for African Americans. For example, race restrictive housing covenants were barriers to African Americans' spatial mobility.[20] At the local level, cities enacted racial

14 Supra Note 10, Plessy, at 551. "We consider the underlying fallacy of the plaintiff's argument to consist in the assumption that the enforced separation of the two races stamps the colored race with a badge of inferiority. If this be so, it is not by reason of anything found in the act, but solely because the colored race chooses to put that construction upon it. The argument necessarily assumes that if, as has been more than once the case, and is not unlikely to be so again, the colored race should become the dominant power in the state legislature, and should enact a law in precisely similar terms, it would thereby relegate the white race to an inferior position. We imagine that the white race, at least, would not acquiesce in this assumption. The argument also assumes that social prejudices may be overcome by legislation, and that equal rights cannot be secured to the negro except by an enforced commingling of the two races. We cannot accept this proposition."

15 Brown v. Board of Educ., 347 U.S. 483 (1954).

16 Id. at 495.

17 Id. at 483.

18 For e.g. Bailey v Patterson 369 U.S. 31 (1962) (1962) prohibiting racial segregation of interstate and intrastate transportation facilities, Loving v. Virginia 388 U.S. 1 (1967) (invalidating prohibition of interracial marriage in violation of due process and equal protection), Swann v. Charlotte-Mecklenburg Board of Education, 402 U.S. 1, 91 S. Ct. 1267; 28 L. Ed. 2d 554; 1971 U.S. LEXIS 52 (1971) promoting busing to achieve racial integration; It is also noteworthy that it also required multiple presidential executive orders that prohibited racial segregation in the military, in contracting and in employment as well as legislation like The Civil Rights Act of 1957, 1960, 1964, 1965, 1968 and 1987 to address segregation and discrimination in housing, Voting, and employment.

19 Some would argue that it continues today with, for example, erosion of voting rights laws, immigration laws etc.

20 See Michela Zonta, Racial Disparities in Home Appreciation, Center for American Prog-

zoning ordinances in an effort to control the increase of African American population and their residential expansion into all or predominantly white neighborhoods.[21] At the federal level, the Federal Housing Act of 1954 not only ensured and promoted, but also furthered residential segregation on a national scale.[22]

The first chapter in this book recounts the sordid history of racial discrimination in housing opportunities and ownership in America. Chapter II considers the Fair Housing Act of 1968, which was enacted to eliminate discrimination in housing and to thereby reverse the negative effects of law and policy that existed before its enactment. Chapter III examines the impact of the judicial system on housing discrimination. Chapter IV questions whether the sociological goals of the Fair Housing Act—including integration—are attainable in a capitalist economic structure. Chapter V examines our collective notion of "communities of opportunity," a concept designed to help meet the goals of the Fair Housing Act and its actual effects on society in black and white. Chapter VI explores the concept of housing choice, and Chapter VII recommends policies and practices that should help create stronger, more thriving American communities.

---

ress, July 15, 2019, retrieved from https://www.americanprogress.org/issues/economy/reports/2019/07/15/469838/racial-disparities-home-appreciation/

21 Christopher Silver, The Racial Origins of Zoning in American Cities, (A chapter in), Manning Thomas, June and Marsha Ritzdorf eds. Urban Planning and the African American Community: In the Shadows. Thousand Oaks, CA: Sage Publications, 1997

22 Douglas S. Massey & Nancy A. Denton, American apartheid: segregation and the making of the underclass (1993) at 51-54; "One of the many ways the government maintained and perpetuated segregation was through the Federal Housing Authority's and Veteran Affairs' race-based loan programs during the 1940s and 1950s, which facilitated the suburbanization of America along racial lines."

CHAPTER I

America's sordid history of racial discrimination in housing

Throughout our nation's history, African Americans have faced systematic public and private efforts to restrict where they could and could not live in order to isolate them into segregated enclaves. Although counterintuitive, after the abolishment of slavery, residential segregation was not as intense or as concentrated as it is today.[23] Residential segregation began to increase dramatically in the years after the U.S. Supreme Court validated "separate, but equal" racial segregation in its 1896 *Plessy v. Ferguson* decision.[24]

African American economic life in the early 1900s centered on Southern cotton agriculture. African Americans grew cotton under a variety of contracts, institutional arrangements, or were tenant farmers. Records from Southern farms indicate that white and Black farm laborers were paid similar wages, and that white and Black tenant farmers worked under similar contracts for similar rental rates. However, a primary difference was that whites in general, were much more likely to own their land. A similar pattern existed in Southern manufacturing during these years. Among the fairly small number of individuals employed in manufacturing in the South, white and Black workers were often paid comparable wages if they worked at the same job for the same company. However, Blacks were much less likely to hold better-paying skilled jobs, and

---

23 John R. Logan, Racial Segregation in Postbellum Southern Cities: The case of Washington, D.C., Demogr Res. 2017; 36: 1759-1784. Retrieved from https://www.ncbi.nlm.nih.gov/pmc/articles/PMC5783568/ and Joseph P. Williams, Segregation's Legacy, U.S. News & World Report. April 20, 2018. Retrieved from https://www.usnews.com/news/the-report/articles/2018-04-20/us-is-still-segregated-even-after-fair-housing-act

24 Supra Note 10 at 551]

they were more likely to work for lower-paying companies.[25] African Americans grew cotton under a variety of contracts, institutional arrangements, or were tenant farmers. Records from Southern farms indicate that white and Black farm laborers were paid similar wages, and that white and Black tenant farmers worked under similar contracts for similar rental rates. However, a primary difference was that whites in general, were much more likely to own their land.

A similar pattern existed in Southern manufacturing during these years. Among the fairly small number of individuals employed in manufacturing in the South, white and Black workers were often paid comparable wages if they worked at the same job for the same company.[26] African Americans mostly resided in the agricultural southern states, but as job opportunities in industrial northern states opened up, they began migrating beyond the south.[27]

Often referred to as the Great Migration, it chronicled the movement of about six million African Americans out of the rural south to urban centers in the northeast, Midwest and west that occurred between 1916 and 1970. This migration was triggered, in large part, by the social and economic realities of widely discriminatory and strictly enforced "Jim Crow" laws. The southern Jim Crow economic system offered little opportunity to African Americans who were chiefly relegated to low paying sharecropping,[28] physical labor, and service industries. When the Great Migration began, a factory wage in the urban north was three times more than what African Americans could expect to earn working the land in the rural south.[29] While union wages during the period did not

25 Thomas N. Maloney, African Americans in the Twentieth Century, Economic History Association, retrieved from https://eh.net/encyclopedia/african-americans-in-the-twentieth-century/

26 Id

27 The Great Migration. History. March 4, 2010. Retrieved from https://www.history.com/topics/black-history/great-migration#:~:text=The%20Great%20Migration%20was%20the,from%20about%201916%20to%201970.

University of Washington. America' Great Migrations Project. Retrieved from http://depts.washington.edu/moving1/ ; Southern whites migrated during this period also in search of better economic opportunities. Whites moved to states in the Mid-west, including Ohio, Indiana, Michigan and Illinois, while Southern Blacks moved to the northeastern states like New York and New Jersey.

28 Eric Arnesen, Encyclopedia of U.S. Labor and Working-class History, Volume 1, Great Migration. 548-550. Retrieved from https://books.google.com/books?id=zEWsZ81Bd3YC&pg=PA548&lpg=PA548&dq=southern+Jim+Crow+little+opportunity+to+African+Americans+relegated+to+sharecropping&source=bl&ots=zC_3W5r3DK&sig=ACfU3U1JjP7YF-4QJumqVja33HaRjTohCg&hl=en&sa=X&ved=2ahUKEwjCi5uw2r7qAhUMTKwKHTTQBzYQ6AEwBXoECAoQAQ#v=onepage&q=southern%20Jim%20Crow%20little%20opportunity%20to%20African%20Americans%20relegated%20to%20sharecropping&f=false

29 Supra n. 27. History

vary widely by region, the wages available to Blacks in the north were not available to them in the south where they were generally denied the opportunity to work these jobs.[30] "Northern employers in many industries faced strong demand for their products and so had a great need for labor. Their traditional source of cheap labor, European immigrants, dried up in the late 1910s as...World War I interrupted international migration. After the end of the war, new laws limiting immigration to the United States would curtail the flow of European labor. Northern employers thus needed a new source of cheap labor, and they turned to Southern Blacks.[31] Destruction of the cotton crop by the boll weevil, an insect that feeds on cotton plants, and poor weather in some southern states during these years made the new opportunities in the North even more attractive."[32] In order to feed the need for workers during the war, cities in the North and West heavily recruited Southern African Americans with promises of opportunities for success.[33]

The impact of the Great Migration was significant. By the time the Great Migration started, 9 out of every 10 African Americans lived in the South, and 3 out of every 4 lived on farms. By the end of the migratory period in 1970, less than 50% of the country's African Americans lived in the south and only 25% lived in rural communities.[34]

Opportunities in their new communities were tainted by widespread racism. And while generally not mandated by law, as it was in the South, racial segregation was commonly practiced. The racial tensions that existed in the North before the migration were supercharged as Southern Black migration was seen as obtruding on white privileges in housing, schooling, and jobs. White Americans

30 See generally wage and cost of living comparisons during the early 1900s, retrieved from https://fraser.stlouisfed.org/title/union-scale-wages-hours-labor-3912/union-scale-wages-hours-labor-1907-1912-476865?start_page=68

31 Thomas N. Maloney, supra n. 25 stating: Through the 1910s and 1920s, relations between black workers and Northern labor unions were often antagonistic. Many unions in the North had explicit rules barring membership by black workers. When faced with a strike (or the threat of a strike), employers often hired in black workers, knowing that these workers were unlikely to become members of the union or to be sympathetic to its goals. Indeed, there is evidence that black workers were used as strike breakers in a great number of labor disputes in the North in the 1910s and 1920s. Beginning in the mid-1930s, African Americans gained greater inclusion in the union movement. By that point, it was clear that black workers were entrenched in manufacturing, and that any broad-based organizing effort would have to include them.

32 Thomas N. Maloney, supra n. 25

33 Supra n. 27. History

34 Supra n. 27. History.

rejected competition for the nation's bounty instead wanting to secure it all for themselves. In response, African Americans developed and moved into their own neighborhoods.

Also during the same period of the African American migration, almost 20 million whites fled the South moving to cities like New York, Philadelphia, and Boston in the northeast as well as Baltimore, Pittsburgh, St. Louis, and Omaha.[35]

Cities responded to the increasing populations by implementing measures to control the growing African American population and provide new spaces for the growing white populations. One of the things that cities across the nation did to limit Blacks' growth while expanding opportunities for whites was to enact racial zoning ordinances. These ordinances which controlled where people could live based on race effectuated racially segregated communities through various laws and policies that invested in white neighborhoods while disinvesting in African American neighborhoods. "In the early 20th century, a number of cities, particularly border cities like Baltimore, St. Louis, and Louisville, Kentucky, passed zoning ordinances that prohibited African-Americans from moving onto a block that was majority white".[36] "The main justification they used was that segregation was necessary because if African-Americans lived in the communities, the property values of those neighborhoods would decline." But, in fact, the Federal Housing Administration's (FHA) own research demonstrated that property values actually rose when African-Americans moved into white neighborhoods. The government chose to ignore its own research in order to perpetuate segregation.[37] The FHA's intentional disregard of its data is an indictment of the government's complicity in systemic racial segregation, particularly in housing.[38]

---

35 James N. Gregory, The Southern Diaspora: How the Great Migrations of White and Black Southerners Transformed America, Univ. of No Carolina press, 2005

36 Katie Nodjimbadem, The racial Segregation of American Cities was anything but Accidental, the Smithsonian magazine, May 30, 2017, retrieved from https://www.smithsonianmag.com/history/how-federal-government-intentionally-racially-segregated-american-cities-180963494/ and see John Kimble, Insuring Inequality: The Role of the Federal Housing Administration in the Urban Ghettoization of African Americans, Law & Social Inquiry, Vol 32, No. 2 (Spring, 2007), pp. 399-434 publ. Wiley on behalf of the American Bar Foundation retrieved from https://www.jstor.org/stable/20108708 citing Luigi Laurenti, Effects of Nonwhite Purchases on Market Prices. The Appraisal Journal, 20(3) and see Thomas L. Gillette, A Study of the Effects of Negro Invasion on Real Estate Values, The American Journal of Economics and Sociology, Vol. 16, No. 2 (Jan., 1957), pp.151-162 retrieved from https://www.jstor.org/stable/3484415

37 Nodjimbadem Id.

38 John Kimble, supra n. 36

In 1934, the FHA explicitly and intentionally supported and promoted segregation by adopting policies and procedures that systematically denied African Americans access to home financing and to higher quality communities.[39]

If government actions had been passive, the segregated residential landscape that exists today might have materialized much differently. But the government, especially through the FHA, was anything but passive. Instead, the FHA was at the forefront of discriminating against African Americans in the housing markets because of their race.

The segregation institutionalized by slavery, along with the government's endorsement of racially discriminatory policies, engrained into American society and housing markets racist assumptions as well as negative and untrue stereotypes of African Americans.[40]

The systematic and consistent denial of African Americans to move about freely in this country has resulted in the firm grip that residential segregation holds in American society. In order to successfully counter residential segregation, we must acknowledge both the dual housing system which operates to

---

39 U.S. COMMISSION ON CIVIL RIGHTS, UNDERSTANDING FAIR HOUSING 1 (1973). (stating that by the time the Federal Government became involved in the housing market in the 1930's the discriminatory policies were already in place. In creating the policies and practices for the newly created federal programs the Federal Government chose to adopt the discriminatory practices used in the private industry.); U.S. Fed. Hous. Admin., *Underwriters Manual* (1934) [Hereinafter Underwriters Manual (1934)]:

309. The points of consideration here are the factors which afford protection and preservation of the desirable neighborhood character. Numerous influences can so change the characteristics of a neighborhood that it will become entirely undesirable for residential purposes. *Protection against some adverse influences is obtained by the proper zoning and deed restrictions that prevail in a neighborhood. Other unfavorable actors may exist outside of the neighborhood and cannot be controlled. Published and utilized city planning affords some assistance in preventing the occurrence of adverse influences.* Sometimes the character of a neighborhood may be so well established that it is relatively free from undesirable influences although no zoning or deed restrictions or similar protection may exist. The natural geography of a neighborhood may also be such that adverse influential factors are kept out.

311. *All mortgages on properties in neighborhoods definitely protected in any way against the occurrence of unfavorable influences obtain a higher rating. The possibility of occurrence of such influences within the life of the mortgage would cause a lower rating or disqualification.* The actual rating given must be commensurate with the degree to which the adverse influence occurrence of unfavorable influences obtain a higher rating. The possibility of occurrence of such influences within the life of the mortgage would cause a lower rating or disqualification. The actual rating given must be commensurate with the degree to which the adverse influence occurs or is likely to occur. (emphasis added);

See also Massey and Denton 1993 supra note 22

40 One example of the negative stereotyping is blockbusting, where realtors use the common misbelief that African Americans lower property values to scare white homeowners into selling their houses. These negative stereotypes and racist assumptions have resulted in a racially unequal housing market where African Americans are given different prices, terms or conditions, and overall experiences.

the disadvantage of African Americans and to the distinct advantage of white Americans, as well as the extent of the government's complicity in contributing to and encouraging residential segregation. We must further recognize the significant influence that official actions at every level continue to have in maintaining racial segregation, unequal housing, and financing markets. Residential segregation is a direct result of racially discriminatory laws, policies, and practices, many of which continue to be enforced. Some of the collateral consequences of centuries of racist policies, laws, and practices are clear.[41] Others are opaque, and emerge only when subconscious beliefs are confronted.[42]

In addition to the political, social and legal policies that continue to support racial segregation in housing, prevailing economic theories have also disadvantaged African Americans.

During the late 1800s and early 1900s, the dominant economic theories were free market and *laissez faire*. The United States Supreme Court favored the laissez-faire approach and struck down many state and federal attempts to regulate different market relationships. Laissez faire theorizes that economies must be permitted to run their respective courses without federal interference. This belief is based on the conjecture that all actors in the market are on equal footing. When segregation was enforced by the government, the assumption of laissez-faire was visibly its fatal flaw. At a time when racial segregation was legal, the laissez-faire economic theory allowed for federal, state, and private actors to openly discriminate, including in the housing market. Thus, the application of a laissez-faire theory in a racially segregated America allowed an unequal housing market to develop; and, coupled with lending and investment laws, intensified residential racial segregation.

Centuries of government actions enforcing and assisting racial segregation at all levels reinforced society's pervasive racial divides. Federal policies of the early 1900s, in particular, greatly contributed to creating racially unequal

41 With the concentration of poverty within African American neighborhoods naturally their property values suffered. With a majority of African Americans living in these areas with low property values, negatively impacted the public schools located there. With poorly funded schools and subpar education, African American children were less competitive in the job market. Thus, African Americans were isolated in areas with high poverty rates, low residential property values, poorly funded schools, and high unemployment rates. Racial discrimination being rampant effectively trapped them in this vicious cycle.

42 John A. Powell, Understanding Our New Racial Reality Starts with the Unconscious, Greater Good Magazine. UC Berkeley's Greater Good Science Center. May 19, 2015. retrieved from https://greatergood.berkeley.edu/article/item/understanding_our_new_racial_reality_starts_with_the_unconscious

housing markets that still impact African Americans.[43] For example, federal policies including: (1) government mandated redlining; (2) providing federal subsidies for construction of white communities but not for Blacks; and, (3) enacting regulations and procedures that intentionally excluded African Americans from sharing financial benefits that white Americans enjoyed impaired African Americans' ability to acquire wealth overall.[44] Among the government's dreadful actions was its rejection of African American veterans from taking advantage of general privileges afforded to white veterans, such as were provided for in the G.I. Bill.[45]

With such a dark American history of government-sanctioned racial hatred, it is difficult to lay today's still segregated housing patterns solely at the feet of the very marginally successful Fair Housing Act of 1968 (The "Act"). While the Act is a little more than 50 years old, slavery alone endured for nearly 250 years in American society. From the post reconstruction period to well into the first half of the twentieth century, racial segregation was direct and explicit.[46]

After slavery was abolished following the Civil War, Black Codes were enacted to 'legally' restrict recently freed slaves and Free Blacks' mobility and ability to exercise their constitutional and civil rights.[47] Prior to the enactment of

---

43 U.S. Fed. Hous. Admin., Underwriters Manual (1934): According to the Underwriting Manual the Agents were warned about the points of consideration here are the factors which afford protection and preservation of the desirable neighborhood character. Because the neighborhoods with race restrictive covenants or racial zoning ordinances were rated higher and those with the possibility of infiltration by one of an undesired race or nationality were rated lower or altogether disqualified in practice it had the effect of excluding African Americans. They were either excluded by the protective measures of race restrictive covenants and racial zoning ordinances or were denied credit.

44 U.S. Fed. Hous. Admin., Underwriters Manual (1934): In the 1934 Underwriting Manual there was segment on "Protection from Adverse Influences" in three paragraphs it detailed points for agents to consider such as whether the neighborhood was protected from "adverse influences" with "proper zoning" or neighborhood deed restrictions. It further warned agents of the ingress of undesirable racial or nationals as "The more important among the adverse influential factors." And, finally it detailed the rating system which would give the highest rating to "mortgages on properties in neighborhoods definitely protected in any way against the occurrence of unfavorable influences." In contrast neighborhoods with "The possibility of occurrence of such influences within the life of the mortgage would cause a lower rating or disqualification." similar provisions can be seen in the Underwriting Manuals of 1936, 1938, 1946.

45 See, generally, Erin Blakemore, How the GI Bill's Promise was denied to a million black WWII Veterans, Sept. 30, 2019, History Stories retrieved from https://www.history.com/news/gi-bill-black-wwii-veterans-benefits

46 Library of Congress. Brown v. Board at Fifty: "With an Even Hand". retrieved from https://www.loc.gov/exhibits/brown/brown-segregation.html

47 Slavery had played such a pivotal role in the souths economic structure up until the civil war that black codes were enacted to replicate the pre-civil war economic system under the disguise of free-

the Act, the right to choose where to live was not protected and often gave way to restrictions on the right to alienate property. The Black Codes were designed to limit African American's freedom and effectuate a continued system of racial inferiority.[48] [49] Under Black Codes, African Americans' right to own land was restricted, they could not bear arms, and they were subjected to possible servitude for vagrancy and other impractical offenses.[50] Black Codes were superseded by *de jure segregation, which brought racial segregation to the national stage.*[51] *De jure* segregation is segregation by public policy, by government law or regulation, not the accidental or occasional incidences of rogue public officials but consistent systematic public policy. Residential segregation is the intentional, malicious result of systematic public policy and should be subject to constitutional remedy.[52]

---

labor system. A Louisiana city had a black ordinance that limited African Americans to work of "some white person"

"Police Regulations of Saint Landry Parish, Louisiana (1865)." Dictionary of American History. Encyclopedia.com. 19 Apr. 2018 <http://www.encyclopedia.com>.

"SECTION 4. Be it further ordained, that every negro is required to be in the regular service of some white person, or former owner, who shall be held responsible for the conduct of said negro. But said employer or former owner may permit said negro to hire his own time by special permission in writing, which permission shall not extend over seven days at any one time. Any negro violating the provisions of this section shall be fined five dollars for each offence, or in default of the payment thereof shall be forced to work five days on the public road, or suffer corporeal punishment as hereinafter provided."

Slavery had been a pillar of economic stability in the region before the war; now, black codes ensured the same stability by recreating the antebellum economic structure under the façade of a free-labor system

48 The Editors of Encyclopaedia Britannica, Black Code, retrieved from https://www.britannica.com/topic/black-code

49 History.com Editors, Black Codes, October 10, 20019 retrieved from https://www.history.com/topics/black-history/black-codes

50 The Editors of Encyclopaedia Britannica, Reconstruction and the New South, 1865-1900 Reconstruction, 1865-1877, retrieved from https://www.britannica.com/place/United-States/Reconstruction-and-the-New-South-1865-1900

51 Congressional Bills 111th Congress. S. Con. Res. 26. U.S. Government Publishing Office. Concurrent Resolution. Retrieved from https://www.govinfo.gov/content/pkg/BILLS-111sconres26es/html/BILLS-111sconres26es.htm ;

Plessy v. Ferguson and the Roots of Segregation. retrieved from http://database.civics.unc.edu/files/2012/05/PlessyvFergusonPPT.pdf ; Kerri L. Hunkele, Segregation in United States Healthcare: From Reconstruction to Deluxe Jim Crow, University of New Hampshire Scholars' Repository. Spring 2014. retrieved from https://scholars.unh.edu/cgi/viewcontent.cgi?article=1189&context=honors

52 Erik Moshe, How the Government Deliberately Segregated Americans by Race, Opinion, Newsweek, Dec 26, 2017 retrieved from https://www.newsweek.com/how-government-deliberately-segregated-americans-race-693752

The housing market and its related industries generally relied on a free market or laissez-faire economic theory and operated free from governmental intrusion—except when it came to maintaining racially segregated communities.

Residential segregation is the intentional byproduct of racial discrimination in the housing market and financing system. At the most basic level, racial discrimination originates from the racist stereotypes and assumptions that centuries of governmental actions have embedded into our society. Countering racial discrimination is an extremely difficult task because of the many interconnected actors that have contributed and reinforced its perpetuation over most of our nation's existence. Slavery, Black Codes, *de jure* segregation, racial zoning ordinances, and race restrictive covenants not only created residential barriers segregating African Americans, but also ensured the strengthening of racial stereotypes by their continuous application.

The Fair Housing Act of 1968[53]: The Good, the Bad Ugly, and the Ugly

53 The Fair Housing Act of 1968 (FHA) (42U.S.C.A. §§ 3601-3631) is also known as Title VIII of the civil rights act of 1968.

CHAPTER 2
The Good

LEGISLATING FAIRNESS

Congress was the last of the three branches to respond to the Civil Rights Movement.[54] The Supreme Court led the way with its landmark decisions in *Warley*,[55] *Shelley*, [56] and *Loving v. Virginia*,[57] giving substantial meaning to the broad constitutional mandates of the Equal Protection Clause of the Fourteenth Amendment and the Due Process Clause of the Fifth Amendment. The Supreme Court reached its limits in two cases. First, in *Brown v. Board of Education*,[58] wherein the Court ordered the desegregation of public schools and again in *Cooper v. Aaron*,[59] where the Court ruled that state laws opposing integration conflicted with the Constitution.[60]

Although the Supreme Court continued to decide constitutionality issues, enforcement of the rulings was the responsibility of the executive branch. It followed the Supreme Court's lead, by enforcing judicial decisions and by issuing executive orders centered on prohibiting federal discrimination.[61] Congress

54 See Federal Civil Rights Enforcement Effort. A Report of The United States Commission on Civil Rights 1970 at 1.

55 245 US 60 (1917).

56 334 US 1 (1948).

57 Supra Note 18. 388 US 1 (1967).

58 347 U.S. 483 (1954).

59 Cooper v. Aaron, 358 U.S. 1.

60 5 U.S. 137 (1803).

61 Executive Order 9808, establishing the president's committee on civil rights, 10925; Executive Order

responded by enacting laws to address constitutional protections. But, in 1957, when Congress adopted civil rights legislation, it failed to take on housing discrimination and would not do so for another ten years.

One of the greatest challenges to curative fair housing legislation was the subject matter itself. Housing regulation contemplates a broad area fraught with emotion, family ties, and personal proclivities that affect almost every American. Enactment of curative housing legislation would cure the ills of restrictive laws while also simultaneously restricting property owners' right to freely alienate their property.

Timing exacerbated these challenges. With the enactment of the Civil Rights Act (CRA) of 1964 and the Voting Rights Act (VRA) of 1965, the central components of the Civil Rights Movement had been achieved, and as a result, the movement began to wind down. Congress, complacent with these achievements, became hesitant to push further civil rights legislation for fear of isolating white Americans. But in 1966, President Johnson submitted a follow-up bill centered on fair housing to Congress, known as the Civil Rights Act of 1966. Johnson was unable to persuade Congress to enact the law and it was killed by filibuster.[62] By then the president's popularity had declined, partly as a result of the United States' involvement in the Vietnam War, which he escalated in the summer of 1965. The war became a priority and the president's civil rights bill was sidelined. At the same time American discontent with Vietnam reached a high point causing Congress to begin pulling its support. An unintended effect of the Vietnam War was that it increased African American consciousness. Vietnam forced African Americans to face the irony of their situation—an irony that befell them during all the previous wars they had fought, fighting for freedom and democracy abroad when they themselves did not enjoy either at home. Soldiers returned home greeted with the same discrimination they had experienced before they left and as African Americans' frustrations reached their limit, their discontent erupted, often violently, in racial dissension across the country. Ironically, as violence escalated, Congress became increasingly hesitant to take further action to enact civil rights legislation.

9981 desegregating the military; Executive Order 10925 creating the Equal Employment Opportunities Commission; Executive order 11246 created nondiscriminatory requirements in government employment and in employment by governmental contractors or subcontractors.

62 HR 14765,

KERNER REPORT

President Johnson established the National Advisory Commission on Civil Disorders (Kerner Commission) in an effort to better understand the source for the widespread civil unrest.[63] Based on reports from earlier civil rights commissions, it was becoming obvious that the denial of spatial assimilation had concentrated and isolated African Americans in America's declining inner cities. Meanwhile, communities outside the inner cities were prospering. In order to remedy the situation, the Kerner report found that Congress would need to remove barriers that were impeding African Americans from moving freely outside of the urban core. Among other things, it meant prohibiting the systemic discriminatory acts and practices that ensured residential segregation. For Americans, the right to freely convey one's property historically had been regarded as an absolute right—a right that prevailed even over one's right to choose where to live. Regulating the housing market therefore meant prioritizing the right to choose where to live over the right to freely alienate property. In passing the prohibitions, Congress would be implicitly placing a limit on the right to freely convey property. It would not be easily accomplished.

LYNDON BAINES JOHNSON

President Johnson, who had built an impressive civil rights track record during his presidency, was an important ally of fair housing legislation. Johnson had played an integral part in the passage of the Civil Rights Act of 1957, the Civil Rights Act of 1960, the Civil Rights Act of 1964, and the Voting Rights Act of 1965.[64]

As a politician from the state of Texas, Johnson had personally witnessed extreme levels of poverty and their consequences during his time teaching Mexican-American children at a segregated school in Cotulla.[65] While Johnson was a pivotal player in enacting the United States' first civil rights act in almost

63 Exec. Order No. 11,365, 3 C.F.R. 674 (Comp. 1967)

64 But see Bruce Bartlett, Wrong on Race: The Democratic Party's Buried Past, where the author discusses the motives behind Johnson's support and his complex history on matters of race

65 Cotulla is a predominately Hispanic (85%) city located in LaSalle County, Texas about 100 miles southwest of San Antonio.

a century in 1957; and it's subsequent, stronger civil rights acts, he had voted against civil rights legislation during his first twenty years in political office.[66]

As president, however, Johnson, unlike his predecessor John F. Kennedy, was an insider, who was very familiar with the complex inner workings of Congress. Johnson had been senate majority leader for years before he was elected vice president. As senate majority leader he was responsible for pushing legislation through Congress and sharpened his negotiating skills and formed close relationships with both Democrats and Republicans in the House of Representatives and Senate. These experiences and relationships proved pivotal in his successful push for the passage of the civil rights bills, including the Civil Rights Act of 1964.

CRA OF 1964

> *"We have talked long enough in this country about equal rights. We have talked for 100 years or more. It is time now to write the next chapter, and to write it in the books of law."*
>
> — *Lyndon B. Johnson*[67]

President John Fitzgerald Kennedy submitted a civil rights bill to Congress in June of 1963 which immediately encountered intense opposition. As the bill was being held up in the Rules Committee, Vice President Johnson worked for the bill's passage with Robert Kennedy; Johnson to lead the fight on Capitol Hill while Kennedy fought to resolve the procedural obstacles. After JFK's assassination, Johnson threw all his weight into getting the civil rights act passed. Upon being sworn in as president, Johnson immediately contacted civil rights

66 Johnson did show signs of sympathy for minorities helping out Austin's African Americans, Mexicans, and White slum dwellers by securing federal funding for housing in 1938. Additionally, Johnson declined to sign the Southern Manifesto which urged resistance to school integration that stemmed from the Supreme Courts Brown v. Board of Education 1954 decision; Civil Rights Act of 1957. Pub. L. No. 85-315, 71 Stat. 634.

67 President Lyndon B. Johnson addressing a joint session of Congress. retrieved from https://www.senate.gov/artandhistory/history/common/generic/CivilRightsAct1964.htm#:~:text=In%20his%20address%2C%20Johnson%20declared,of%20the%20bill%2C%20HR%207152.

leaders, rallying their support and cooperation. Johnson also worked with Everett Dirksen, the Senate minority leader, asking for his assistance in marshaling Republican Party support. Johnson convinced the nation that the best way to honor the recently assassinated President John Kennedy was to pass the civil rights bill.

Johnson got the civil rights bill out of the Rules Committee, a required stop where civil rights bills often go to die, by threatening to use a discharge petition to circumvent the committee and move the bill onto the floor.[68] The strategy worked. Fearing being ridiculed by being overridden, the Rules Committee released the bill and it was shortly approved once it arrived onto the floor. At the Senate, a filibuster remained the last obstacle for the civil rights bill. The filibuster was a tactic that Southern congresspersons often used to stymie civil rights legislation. Johnson overcame the threat of a filibuster by convincing Republican leader Everett Dirksen to support the bill. Dirksen, along with Democratic Senator Hubert Humphrey gathered the votes necessary to invoke cloture which put an end to the filibuster. Cloture occurs when the Senate votes to place a time limit on consideration of a bill thereby overcoming the prolonged debate by filibuster.

THE CIVIL RIGHTS ACT OF 1964

In less than a year, Johnson had managed to get the 1964 Civil Rights bill enacted into law. On the high note of the passage, Johnson was nominated as Democratic Party's presidential candidate for the 1964 presidential election which he won in a landslide victory. His momentum carried over to the Congressional elections where the Democrats won many of the seats. The 89th Congress saw the Democratic party enjoy a powerful greater than two-to-one majority.[69] Armed

---

68 If a majority of House members sign a discharge petition, a bill is taken from the committee, to the chagrin of its chairman. Johnson made the petition his own personal crusade. Even Risen credits his zeal, noting that after receiving a list of 22 House members vulnerable to pressure on the petition, the president immediately ordered the White House switchboard to get them on the phone, wherever they could be found. Johnson engaged an army of lieutenants—businessmen, civil-rights leaders, labor officials, journalists, and allies on the Hill—to go out and find votes for the discharge petition.

69 The Democratic advantage had been sixty-eight to thirty-two until April 30, 1966, when Michigan Democrat Patrick V. McNamara died and was replaced by Republican Robert P. Griffin.

with widespread support, Johnson enacted the Social Security Amendments Act and Voting Rights Act of 1965 (VRA) within his first year in office.

THE CIVIL RIGHTS ACT OF 1966

The Civil Rights Act of 1966 was a major piece of fair housing legislation that passed the House, but failed in the Senate. Even though the Democrats had a two-thirds majority in both the House and Senate, many representatives feared that supporting fair housing legislation would cost them the support of their core white constituents. Unable to garner the support he had achieved previously for the passage of the Civil Rights Act of 1964 and the subsequent Voting Rights Act of 1965, fair housing proved to be too divisive, and ultimately broke up Johnson's civil rights coalition.[70] With the collapse of this coalition, the 1966 bill was left vulnerable to a filibuster in the Senate. [71]

90TH CONGRESS

Two years after Johnson's landslide presidential victory, the Democrats lost many seats in the 1966 midterm elections.[72] When the 90th Congressional second session opened, H.R. 2516, a minimal civil rights bill, was introduced. This bill immediately encountered a filibuster from a unified Southern front.[73] In response to the South's opposition to the weak civil rights bill, Minnesota Democratic Senator Walter Mondale and Massachusetts Republican Senator

---

70 "An unlikely coalition had come together on the Rules Committee, of liberal Democrats, led by Vice President Hubert Humphrey, moderate and liberal Republicans, led by Senator Everett Dirksen and a single conservative midwesterner, Republican Clarence Brown of Ohio. Brown controlled enough GOP votes to force Smith's hand by threatening to wrest control of the committee from him. Rather than face that loss of power and resulting humiliation, Smith agreed to hold hearings on civil rights in early January." see National Archives retrieved from https://www.archives.gov/publications/prologue/2004/summer/civil-rights-act-2.html

71 112 Cong. Rec. S23,042-43 (daily ed. Sept. 19, 1966) (Senate cloture vote on H.R. 14765, Civil Rights Act of 1966)

72 Walter Mondale recalled that despite the midterm losses, "We had a pretty good Senate." Interview with Walter Mondale, former United States Vice President and Senator, in Minneapolis, Minn. (July 15, 2009).

73 Senator Ervin of North Carolina led the filibuster against H.R. 2516.

Edward Brooke co-sponsored S. 1358, a strong fair housing amendment.[74] S.1358 would prohibit discrimination in both the sale and rental of housing, contained strong enforcement provisions, and significant penalties for those found to be in violation of fair housing regulations. Enforcement wise, the bill authorized the Housing and Urban Development (HUD)'s secretary to enforce the regulations by investigating discrimination allegations, issuing complaints against suspected violators and resolving disputes through an internal administrative process wherein hearings could be convened to determine how severe a violation was. Upon a finding of discrimination, HUD could grant relief by issuing cease and desist orders. Furthermore, the bill empowered the United States Attorney General to pursue claims where there was a pattern and practice of racial discrimination.[75]

Four days later, a vote for cloture failed with fifty-five votes in favor and thirty-seven against proceeding to vote.[76] Unable to move forward with other business, Senate Majority and Minority Leaders Mansfield and Dirksen joined to table the legislation.

> "The image of the tumbledown slatboard shack in the rural South has been replaced by what is to my mind an even more regrettable, more terrible alternative—the filthy, freezing urban slum tenement. Added to the monumental problem of poverty in the cities is the totally related problem of segregated housing. These two monstrous national disgraces are really only one."
>
> Senator Walter F. Mondale 82

74 114 CONG. REC. S3235–53 (1968); The reasoning was simple, if a weak civil rights bill was going to face the intense Southern opposition, liberals might as well put forth a strong one and try to circumvent the filibuster with votes from Northern Republicans. Mondale interview, supra note 72.

75 See Metcalf, George R. 1988. Fair Housing Comes of Age. New York: Greenwood.

76 At the time, Senate Rules required two-thirds of members present and voting to invoke cloture. See Richard S. Beth, Cong. Research Serv., Rl32878, Cloture Attempts on Nominations: Data and Historical Development 6 (2013).

COMPROMISE

In order to draw the support needed to invoke cloture, the bill was amended to reduce its coverage to eighty percent of the housing market. The amended bill excluded houses sold by owners without the use of public advertising or a broker. The compromise also weakened the bill's enforcement provisions. For example, the power to enforce the new requirements was reassigned to the Department of Justice (DOJ) and the penalties were reduced.[77] Further, HUD's authority to hold hearings, issue complaints, and publish cease and desist orders were eliminated.

KERNER REPORT RELEASED

On March 1, 1968, while the Senate was in the middle of a filibuster against the Mondale-Brooke co-sponsored civil rights bill, and shortly after the Mansfield-Dirksen compromise, the Kerner Report was released. The Report made bold conclusions and ultimately warned that the nation was "moving toward two societies, one black, one white--separate and unequal."[78] The report found that African Americans dealt with many issues, such as police bias and brutality [79] that were foreign to their white counterparts.[80] The report concluded that the leading causes for civil disorders were segregation and white racism.[81] The years of policies enforcing segregation at every level had created a vicious cycle of poverty that trapped many African Americans. First, African American populations were concentrated in the inner cities as a result of having been excluded from many of the federal benefits and mortgage subsidies.[82] Second, the con-

77 Mondale interview, supra note 72. Senator Mondale knew of Senator Dirksen's dislike for new bureaucracies stating, "Dirksen didn't want new bureaucracies,"

78 Nat'l Advisory Comm'n on Civil Disorders, Report of the Commission on Civil Disorders vi (1968) [hereinafter Kerner Report]

79 Id. at 8 (The abrasive relationship between the police and minority communities has been a major: ----and explosive---source. of grievance, tension, and disorder. The blame must be shared by the total society.)

80 Id. at 1

81 Id. at 1. (Discrimination and segregation have long permeated much of American life; they now threaten the future of every American.)

82 Id at 6. (Almost all Negro population growth (96 percent from 1950 to 1966) is occurring within

struction of low-income housing only in predominantly African American neighborhoods created a negative economic domino effect. African American property, which was already appraised at artificially low values by creditors, saw those values further diminished by the concentration of low-income housing in already marginalized communities.[83] Another major consequence of the historical discrimination was poorly funded schools, as many public schools are funded through property taxes. With the combination of low-income families and declining property values, funding for public schools dropped. The report showed that African American students who went to the inadequately funded schools often suffered from poor resources which resulted in diminished education quality. As a result of receiving lower quality education, they became less competitive in the job market, leading to higher unemployment rates[84] and violence. The Kerner Report recommended the "[e]nactment of a national comprehensive and enforceable open occupancy law."[85]

The timing of the Kerner Report, along with its focus on the effects of racial segregation as a leading cause of two unequal and racially separate societies,

---

metropolitan areas, primarily within central cities.)

83 Andre Perry, Jonathan Rothwell and David Harshbarger, The Devaluation of Assets in Black Neighborhoods, November 2018 retrieved from https://www.brookings.edu/wp-content/uploads/2018/11/2018.11_Brookings-Metro_Devaluation-Assets-Black-Neighborhoods_final.pdf stating that "Homes of similar quality in neighborhoods with similar amenities are worth 23 percent less in majority black neighborhoods, compared to those with very few or no black residents. Majority black neighborhoods do exhibit features associated with lower property values, including higher crime rates, longer commute times, and less access to high-scoring schools and well-rated restaurants. Yet, these factors only explain roughly half of the undervaluation of homes in black neighborhoods. Across all majority black neighborhoods, owner-occupied homes are undervalued by $48,000 per home on average, amounting to $156 billion in cumulative losses. Homes of similar quality in neighborhoods with similar amenities are worth 23 percent less in majority black neighborhoods, compared to those with very few or no black residents. Majority black neighborhoods do exhibit features associated with lower property values, including higher crime rates, longer commute times, and less access to high-scoring schools and well-rated restaurants. Yet, these factors only explain roughly half of the undervaluation of homes in black neighborhoods. Across all majority black neighborhoods, owner-occupied homes are undervalued by $48,000 per home on average, amounting to $156 billion in cumulative losses."

84 Id. at 6 (Employment is a key problem. It not only controls the present for the Negro American but, in a most profound way, it is creating the future as well. Yet, despite continuing economic growth and declining national unemployment rates, the unemployment rate for Negroes in 1967 was more than double that for whites.)

(This concentration of male Negro employment at the lowest end of the occupational scale is the single most important cause of poverty among Negroes)

85 Supra n.78 at 11. "The major goal is the creation of a true union-a single society and a single American identity."

helped strengthen support for the civil rights housing measure.[86] After the release of the Report, several Republican senators switched their earlier, resistant positions and agreed to support the bill. On March 4, 1968, the bill's co-sponsors had garnered the required two-thirds Senate vote to invoke cloture of debate. After the Fair Housing Act (The Act) cleared the Senate, it was then sent to the House where it faced Southern opposition and the possibility of being weakened. The bill was remanded to the Rules Committee where it was held up, and by the adjournment of the House on April 4, 1968, its future appeared uncertain. Later that day the Rev. Dr. Martin Luther King Jr. was assassinated, and his shocking death changed the trajectory of the bill. His assassination materialized the warnings of the Kerner Report and saw African American frustrations climax into riots across the nation. As Congress observed the dramatic shifting of the nation's mood, about twenty-one House Representatives broke party ranks in support of the Senate's Fair Housing Senate bill. [87] The bill passed immediately in the Senate; and on April 10, 1968, the House passed the bill. The following day President Johnson signed the Fair Housing Act into law.

The Act was a step toward addressing the issue of residential segregation.[88] It proscribed discriminatory practices in the housing and financing markets that had for so long ensured racially segregated communities and unequal opportunities.[89]

---

86 Susan T. Gooden and Samuel L. Myers, Jr., The Kerner Commission Report Fifty Years Later: Revisiting the American Dream, RSF: The Russell Sage Foundation Journal of the Social Sciences, retrieved from https://www.rsfjournal.org/content/rsfjss/4/6/1.full.pdf

87 42 U.S.C. §§ 3601-19, 3631 (1994 & Supp. I 1995). The Fair Housing Act was originally enacted as Title VIII of the Civil Rights Act of 1968, and was augmented by the Fair Housing Amendments Act of 1988, Pub. I. No. 100-420, 102 Stat. 1619. [Hereinafter the FHA]

88 See, e.g., Christopher Bonastia, Knocking On The Door: The Federal Government's Attempt To Desegregate The Suburbs 87(2006) ("Most observers agree that King's death was critically important in gathering sufficient support for the 1968 fair housing legislation."); John Goering, Introduction and Overview to Fragile Rights Within Cities: Government, Housing, And Fairness 1, 9 (John Goering ed., 2007) (arguing that the Fair Housing Act did not transfer sufficient authority to the federal government partially "because a motivation for the law's enactment was major urban riots following the murder of Martin Luther King on April 4, 1968."

89 42 U.S.C. § 3604 (2000). The Act made three major impacts on the housing marketplace: a) it prohibited sellers and renters from discriminating in transactions; b) it forbade intermediary actors such as real estate agents and mortgage brokers from discriminating in their facilitation of transactions; and c) it commanded the federal government to affirmatively promote fair housing.

The enactment of the Act was an iconic moment in American history, marking Congress' affirmative actions to address residential segregation that plagued the nation. The Act was a promise, especially to African Americans, that they would be afforded equal access to an important piece of the American dream—home ownership. It promised to diminish acts of housing discrimination by individuals and entities when it came to purchasing, leasing, and financing homes; and to foster racially integrated residential communities.[90]

To transition from the systemic acts of discrimination in housing, whether explicit or implicit, the Act identifies prohibited housing practices including sales, rentals, advertising, and financing. The Fair Housing Act broadly rejected discriminatory practices in real estate transactions, sales and rentals, sales relationships within the profession and real estate financing and insurance and provided means to enforce the Act's bans.

The Act made it unlawful to refuse to sell, rent to, or negotiate with any person because of race, color, religion, sex, familial status, handicap, or national origin.[91] Generally, the Act prohibits discrimination in the sale or rental of a dwelling because of the race, color, religion, sex, familial status, handicap, or national origin or disability of: (1) the buyer or renter, (2) a person who will reside in the dwelling after it is sold or rented, or (3) any person associated with the buyer or renter.[92]

The Act also prohibits discriminatory advertising practices in the sale or rental of housing.[93] Even unpublished statements that include discriminatory expressions and conduct could violate the act. In cases, for example, where landlords instructed agents or employees not to rent to African Americans or conversely to give preference to whites, such acts of discrimination and preference violated the Act.[94]

---

90 Fair Housing Act, 42 USC 3604 § 804

91 The Fair Housing Amendments Act of 1988 added extensive provisions that apply to discrimination against disabled persons and families with children 18 years of age and under.

92 42 U.S.C. 3604(f)(1)(A-C)

93 42 U.S.C. §3604

94 Corey v. Secretary, U.S. Dept. of Housing & Urban Development ex rel. Walker, 719 F.3d 322 (USCA-4th, 2013); Greater New Orleans Fair Housing Action Center v. Kelly, 364 F.Supp.3d 635 (E.D. La, 2019).

The law is designed to thwart owners and their agents from misrepresenting that a dwelling is unavailable for inspection, rental, or sale, when, in fact, it actually is available.[95] In one case, the court found that a realty firm that posted "sold" signs on the lawn of a white seller in a white neighborhood in an attempt to steer minorities away from purchasing houses in the neighborhood had violated the Act.[96]

The Fair Housing Act also sought to end blockbusting. Blockbusting may be actionable even when the sales person believes (s)he is merely advising the seller or purchaser if the salesman acts out on either's fear in order to keep minorities out of or direct them to a particular neighborhood.[97]

Real estate professionals may also seek protection under the Act when they are harmed by the discriminatory actions of their client as in Williams vs. Miller.[98] In that case, realtors sued the seller for refusing to sell to an African American couple.

The Fair Housing Act also governs the housing financing industry and prohibits discrimination in the financing of housing transactions including property appraisals.[99] As broad as the Act is, it does not include every action that sounds in discrimination and certain categories of real estate transactions are specifically excepted including some religious organizations, private clubs, and senior housing.

---

95 Donald Trump and his father were accused by many of telling their agents and employees not to rent to African Americans. One such instance occurred in July 1972 at the Trumps' Shore Haven properties in Brooklyn, when an African American woman sought to rent an apartment. The superintendent turned her away, informing her that nothing was available. A short time later, a white woman applied, and the same superintendent told her she could immediately rent one of two apartments that were available for rent.

The Trumps' persistent patterns of racial discrimination in housing served as the inspiration for several songs against racism that Guthrie witnessed while a tenant in a Brooklyn apartment building that Fred Trump owned. Guthrie's "Old Man Trump" attacks Trump for refusing to rent to African Americans and other minorities and stirring the racial hatred. The lyrics were written in 1954 and found after Guthrie's death. They are on display in the Woody Guthrie Center in Tulsa, Oklahoma. See Petula Dvorak, 'Racial Hate': A famed folk singer, Trump's dad and angry lyrics at a Tulsa landmark, The Washington Post, June 20, 2020 retrieved from https://www.washingtonpost.com/history/2020/06/20/woody-guthrie-fred-trump-tulsa-lyrics/

96 Sanders v. Dorris, 873 F.2d 938 (CA-6th Circ., 1989)

97 Racial Steering: The Real Estate Broker and Title VIII, 85 Yale L.J. 808, 810-818 (Note, May 1976)

98 460 F. Supp. 761 (N.D. Illinois-Eastern, 1978)

99 42 U.S.C. 3605

CHALLENGES TO THE ACT

A law is only as strong as its enforcement provisions allow. Under the original Fair Housing Act, a private citizen could file a civil lawsuit in federal court against the alleged violator or the Attorney General could file a civil suit when there is evidence of a violator's pattern or practice of housing discrimination. When the Attorney General prevailed in these types of lawsuits, the Act allowed the awarding of injunctive relief and monetary damages to the aggrieved party. In addition, the Court could assess civil penalties against the violator up to $50,000 for a first violation, and up to $100,000 for any subsequent violations. There is no question that the law originally intended to include strong enforcement measures but political maneuvering cost the Act some of its teeth. The Dirksen compromise weakened the Act's charge that the HUD Secretary would "administer the programs and activities relating to housing and urban development in a manner affirmatively to further the policies [of the Act]."[100] The Dirksen compromise not only reduced the bill's coverage, but also severely weakened its enforcement provisions. Even though HUD continued to be the agency responsible for the Act's implementation, the Department of Justice was the enforcer. This bifurcated structure radically stripped HUD's ability to ensure compliance by using hearings, issuing complaints, and issuing cease and desist orders. Moreover, while HUD was empowered to investigate claims of discrimination it had only thirty days to decide whether to pursue a claim. If HUD decided to pursue a claim, the agency was able to engage only in "conference, conciliation, and persuasion."[101] Further, HUD was instructed to redirect claims of discrimination if they occurred in a state with a "substantially equivalent" fair housing statute, to that state's authorities. Even if HUD referred a case to the Department of Justice, Section 814 of the Act provides:

> Whenever the Attorney General has reasonable cause to believe that any person or group of persons is engaged in a *pattern or practice* of resistance to the full enjoyment of any of the rights granted by this subchapter, or that any group of persons has been denied any of the rights granted by this subchapter and such denial raises an issue of general public importance, *he* may bring a civil action in any appropriate United States district court by filing with it a

100 42 U.S.C. §§ 3608(c), (d) (1970).

101 42 U.S.C. §3610 (a) (1970)

> complaint setting forth the facts and requesting such preventive relief, including an application for a permanent or temporary injunction, restraining order, or other order against the person or persons responsible for such pattern or practice or denial of rights, as *he* deems necessary to insure the full enjoyment of the rights granted by this subchapter. *Emphasis added*

In other words, even if discrimination was found, the Attorney General could act only if either there was evidence of a pattern or practice or shown an issue of general importance was raised. Patricia R. Harris, former Secretary of HUD, shared her frustration with Congress, testifying that HUD's authority had been reduced to "asking the discovered lawbreaker whether he wants to discuss the matter."[102]

Additionally, the Act mandated strict filing deadlines of either 180 days from the date of the violation or 30 days after the conclusion of mediation with HUD. If suit was filed, the judge was empowered to award actual damages, equitable relief, and attorney's fees to the prevailing party. The judge also may only assess civil penalties against the violators, which could range from $25,000 to $50,000 but could not award punitive damages nor require the violator to take affirmative action to deter continued discrimination.

Moreover, filing suit was additionally burdensome on the losing plaintiff who would be liable for court costs and attorney's fees.

STRENGTHENING THE ACT

There have been several initiatives added to support the Fair Housing Act housing since the Act was passed in 1968. In 1974, the Equal Credit Opportunity Act was passed to make it unlawful for creditors to discriminate against any minority applicant. In 1997, the Community Reinvestment Act was passed in order to encourage financial institutions to help meet the credit needs of borrowers in all segments of their communities, including low income neighborhoods. The additional acts were created to help seal some of the cracks in the original Fair Housing Act, by addressing more specific acts of discrimination including the lack of credit opportunities in low income neighborhoods. However, more than

102 Fair Housing Act: Hearings Before the Subcomm. on Civil and Constitutional Rights of the H. Comm. on the Judiciary, 95th Cong. 30 (1978) (statement of Patricia Roberts Harris, Sec'y, U.S. Dep't of Housing and Urban Dev.) (Emphasis omitted).

a decade after the Act was passed, the 1980 census reported that one-third of African Americans remained in hyper-segregated communities.[103] By the 2010 census, the number had changed only minimally and the pattern of minimal decline continues today.[104]

103 Douglas Massey and Nancy A. Denton, American Apartheid: Segregation and the Making of the Underclass, Harvard University Press. 1993. Massey and Denton, *supra* note 22, at 77 (discussing how no other group in the contemporary United States comes close to this level of isolation). Although Hispanics are considered poor and disadvantaged compared to whites, they do not suffer nearly as much as African Americans from residential isolation. Id.

104 Massey, D.S., Tannen, J. A Research Note on Trends in Black Hypersegregation. *Demography* 52, 1025–1034 (2015). https://doi.org/10.1007/s13524-015-0381-6 and see William H. Frey, Black-White segregation edges downward since 2000, Census shows, Dec. 17, 2018 retrieved from https://www.brookings.edu/blog/the-avenue/2018/12/17/black-white-segregation-edges-downward-since-2000-census-shows/ and see Michael B. Sauter, The most Segregated Cities in America, Special Report, Wall Street journal Feb 20, 2021, retrieved from https://247wallst.com/special-report/2021/02/20/the-most-segregated-cities-in-america/

CHAPTER 3
The Bad

THE FAIR HOUSING ACT: PROMISES OF ELIMINATING HOUSING DISCRIMINATION YET FULFILLED

"I am not your Negro"

James Baldwin

In the months before the Fair Housing Act was passed in 1968, the United States was in the throes of deepening racial tension. The country seemed baffled why, after centuries of horrific mistreatment, untold barbarity and immeasurable suffering, African Americans were angry enough to resort to violence. In July 1967, President Lyndon B. Johnson appointed the National Advisory Commission on Civil Disorders, also known as the Kerner Commission, headed by Illinois governor, Otto Kerner. The commission would ostensibly answer three questions: What happened? Why did it happen? and What can be done to prevent it from happening again? In other words, "What's wrong with our Negroes"?[105]

Television allowed the nation to bear witness to African American men and women being hosed down because they dared to sit at a lunch counter. They

105 See Alice George, The 1968 Kerner Commission Got it Right, But Nobody Listened, Smithsonianmag.com, March 1, 2018 retrieved from https://www.smithsonianmag.com/smithsonian-institution/1968-kerner-commission-got-it-right-nobody-listened-180968318/ wherein the author discusses how inherent in the discussions about African Americans rights is the pervasive white perception and system of values. For example, the report recommended aggressive government spending to provide equal opportunities to African-Americans, but equal rights was not as valued as spending billions to go to the moon. This and similar systems of prioritization and valuations make up an important part of how whites see things, report things and react to things having to do with African Americans. This concept of white perceptions is specifically identified as part of the problem in the Kerner Report. In fact, the idea that white racism caused so many of the negative experiences of African Americans was so unacceptable to the white perspective, not only was there a public backlash to the report but President Johnson himself never accepted the report and implicitly rejected it.

witnessed African American men and women being beaten by policemen with their batons and flashlights. They witnessed African American men and women being savagely dragged in the streets. They watched African American men and women being hauled off to prison for their crime of daring to be equal. Jailed by lawless men who were often following their unconstitutionally unlawful government mandates.

After the Kerner Commission studied the questions for seven months, it published its report February 29, 1968, documenting causes of Black unrest. The report blamed state and federal governments; and also identified failed housing, education, and social service policies as instigating factors that led to the nation's civil unrest. The report also charged mainstream media for having "too long basked in a white world, looking out of it, if at all, with white men's eyes and white perspective."

THE WHITE PERSPECTIVE[106]

The Commission identified one of the main causes of urban violence as white racism, and called for the creation of new jobs for black people, and the end of pervasive *de facto* segregation in major cities. The report recommended the government invest billions of dollars to break up residential segregation and, additionally recommended working toward a more diverse police force and race sensitive police reform.[107]

THE RESILIENCE OF SEGREGATION

Although the Act has been in effect for more than fifty years, residential segregation thrives throughout America. Even as there has been increased racial diversity in America, communities remain racially segregated. While that may be changing, the change is slow. For example, there was a slight decline in residential segregation between Blacks and whites between 1980-2000.[108] That declin-

106 Id.

107 Otto Kerner, The Kerner Report: The 1968 Report of the National Advisory Commission on Civil Disorders, Pantheon; October 12, 1988 ISBN-10 0679720782; ISBN-13: 978-0679720782

108 See U.S. Census Bureau, Racial and Ethnic Residential Segregation in the United States: 1980-2000,

ing trend continued into the next decade, although the pace was sluggish.[109] The overall downward trend in segregation was not reflected across the board, however, as some hyper-segregated neighborhoods not only remained segregated but, showed no signs of integration.[110] Further, the downward trend in residential segregation between Blacks and whites was not followed by other minority groups.[111] Hispanics and non-Hispanic whites, for example, displayed no signs of integration and instead actually experienced increased segregation.[112] The US 2010 Project analyzed 2010 Census information to determine neighborhood segregation levels by quantifying the diversity of average persons within a neighborhood, and then used that information to determine historic segregation patterns in the nation's diversity growth.[113] It found

- that segregation peaked around 1960 or 1970.
- The steady rate of segregation of Hispanic and Asian populations, which, along with their rapid population growth, has resulted in a rise of "intense ethnic enclaves in many parts of the country."[114]
- Segregated communities continue to be overwhelmingly segregated by race.[115]

---

at 4.

109 John R. Logan and Brian Stults. 2011. The Persistence of Segregation in the Metropolis: New Findings from the 2010 Census" Census Brief prepared for Project US2010. http://www.s4.brown.edu/us2010. at 2. [hereinafter referred to as Logan Report]

110 Id

111 Id. at 3.

112 Id. at 10. According to Logan while Hispanics have had had no significant change in their segregation levels, in Metropolitan areas with the largest Hispanic populations the segregation levels were substantially higher. Additionally, while Hispanic segregation in areas where Hispanic presence is new is lower, there was a slight increase.

113 Id. at 1.

114 Id.

115 Aaron Williams and Armand Emamdjomeh, America is more diverse than ever-but still segregated, Washington Post, National Analysis, May 10, 2018 retrieved from https://www.washingtonpost.com/graphics/2018/national/segregation-us-cities/ and see Rakeen Mabud, History and Housing Discrimination: Why Neighborhoods in the United States are Still so Segregated, Forbes Magazine, Dec 4, 2019 retrieved from https://www.forbes.com/sites/rakeenmabud/2019/12/04/history-and-housing-discrimination-why-neighborhoods-in-the-united-states-are-still-so-segregated/#773e61e5501d and see Ann Choi, Keith Herbert, Olivia Winslow and project editor Arthur Browne, Long Island

- The average segregation level fell modestly between 2013-2017 and as widespread segregation declines continue, most areas remain highly segregated.[116]

THE FAIR HOUSING ACT OF 1968: OVERCOMING PAST WRONGS

The Fair Housing Act of 1968 made a broad range of discriminatory practices related to housing unlawful and could have been a powerful tool for plaintiffs to use in order to successfully combat discrimination.[117] Yet, the Department of Justice (DOJ) did not file a single mortgage discrimination case for twenty-three years, until 1991, and private cases were similarly uncommon and particularly difficult to win.[118]

However, enforcement of the Act's prohibition against racial discrimination in mortgage lending received a substantial boost from four laws enacted in the mid-1970s. The Consumer Credit Protection Act ("CCPA") of 1968 to protect consumers against lenders, the Equal Credit Opportunity Act ("ECOA") of 1974 made discrimination within credit transaction processes unlawful;[119] the Home Mortgage Disclosure Act ("HMDA") of 1975 required lenders to publicly disclose

Divided, Nov 17, 2019 retrieved from https://projects.newsday.com/long-island/real-estate-agents-investigation/#open-paywall-message reporting widespread discrimination through racial steering in housing on Long Island New York, with African Americans discriminated against almost 50% of the time while Hispanics and Asians also suffered discrimination but to a lesser degree.

116 See generally, William H Frey, Black-white segregation edges downward since 2000, census shows, The Brookings Institution, Dec 2018 retrieved from https://www.brookings.edu/blog/the-avenue/2018/12/17/black-white-segregation-edges-downward-since-2000-census-shows/

117 42 U.S.C. §§ 3604–3606 (2012). For the purpose of this Comment, § 3605, making it unlawful for "any person or . . . business . . . to discriminate against any person in making available such a transaction . . . because of race" is the most germane section of the FHA; *but see* Cassandra Jones Havard, "On the Take": The Black Box of Credit Scoring and Mortgage Discrimination, 20 B.U. PUB. INT. L.J. 241, 244-45 (2011) (stating that the original fair lending laws are not well suited to combat more complex "second-generation discrimination" of the type we see today).

118 *See* Robert G. Schwemm & Jeffrey L. Taren, *Discretionary Pricing, Mortgage Discrimination, and the Fair Housing Act*, 45 HARV. CIV. RTS. -CIV. LIBERTIES L. REV. 375, 385–90 (2010) (noting that the DOJ did not file a single mortgage discrimination case until the mid-1990s and that private litigants were infrequent and largely unsuccessful); *see also* Nat'l Comm'n on Fair Hous. & Equal Opportunity, The Future of Fair Housing 22–25 (2008) (discussing the lack of enforcement activity in the 2000s).

119 Codified at 15 U.S.C. § 1691(a)(1) (2012) (making it unlawful for any creditor to discriminate against any applicant with respect to any aspect of a credit transaction on the basis of race).

mortgage lending data;[120] and, the Community Reinvestment Act ("CRA") of 1977 specifically sought to curtail redlining practices through regular fair lending examinations.

a. CCPA & ECOA

Discrimination on the basis of race, gender, age, national origin, religion, color, marital status, receipt of public assistance income, and good faith exercise of rights was prohibited under the Consumer Credit Protection Act (CCPA)[121] and the Equal Credit Opportunity Act (ECOA) of 1974.[122] While most of the CCPA is solely applicable to consumer transactions, the ECOA is more broadly applicable to discriminatory practices.[123] The ECOA primarily prohibits credit discrimination[124] on the basis or race and applies to consumer credit, credit transactions involving business or government, and to incidental credit not subject to a finance charge.[125] African American[126] plaintiffs may bring a civil action on the grounds that they were treated less favorably than similarly situated white applicants.[127] Under the ECOA, discrimination can be overt or indirect (neutral on its face, but having a disproportionate impact).[128] It also imposes several affirmative actions on creditors to: (1) provide a copy of an appraisal if the credit

120 Codified at 12 U.S.C. § 2801-2810 (2012). The HMDA did not require lenders to include race and ethnicity until the 1989 amendments to that Act, data from which was not made public until 1994. Dubravka Ritter, *Do We Still Need the Equal Credit Opportunity Act?* (Sept. 2012) FRB of Philadelphia - Payment Cards Center Discussion Paper No. 12-03. Retrieved from https://ssrn.com/abstract=2154865.

121 Pub.L. 90–321, 82 Stat. 146.

122 See generally 15 U.S.C. § 1691-1691f (2006).

123 American Bar Association, "The Consumer Credit Protection Act," 2004, http://apps.americanbar.org/buslaw/newsletter/0024/ materials/book.pdf f

124 *Supra Note 122*

125 Id.

126 And others whose claim is based on disparate treatment because of some constitutionally impermissible reason including ethnicity, national origin

127 *See, e.g., Williams v. First Federal Savings and Loan Ass'n*, 554 F. Supp. 447 (N.D.N.Y. 1981) (the fact that another creditor granted credit to the applicant does not alone establish a violation), *aff'd*, 697 F.2d 302 (2d Cir. 1982); *Markham v. Colonial Mortgage Service Co.*, 605 F.2d 566 (D.C. Cir. 1979) (violation of act to aggregate income of married couples but not of unmarried partners, under circumstances of case).

128 12 CFR § 202.6(a) n.2.

applied for will be secured by a dwelling;[129] (2) supply notice of action taken on an application, and if denial of credit, provide reasons for denial to applicants;[130] and, (3) furnish information on credit transactions.[131]

b. HMDA

In the mid-1970s, Congress enacted the Home Mortgage Disclosure Act (HMDA) to address the issue of discrimination against minority borrowers particularly where they were denied mortgage loans more frequently than white borrowers; and, to determine whether those inconsistencies reflected discrimination in financial institutions' lending practices.[132] At first, mortgage lenders only had to collect and report geographic information on loan originations and purchases to federal regulatory agencies and the general public.[133] Congress amended the HMDA in 1989 to require lenders to collect and report further information about the race, sex, and income of applicants for home mortgage loans.[134] This data constitutes a unique record of the flows of credit in geographic areas of the United States from which the possible presence of discriminatory patterns could be more easily discerned.

c. CRA

The Community Reinvestment Act (CRA)[135] was enacted in 1977 to prevent redlining[136] and encourage banking and savings institutions to help meet the

129 12 CFR § 202.14

130 12 CFR § 202.9

131 12 CFR § 202.10

132 *See generally* Winnie F. Taylor, *Eliminating Racial Discrimination in the Subprime Mortgage Market: Proposals for Fair Lending Reform*, 18 J.L. & Pol'y 263, 281 (2009).

133 Home Mortgage Disclosure Act of 1975 § 304(a).

134 *See* Home Mortgage Disclosure, 54 Fed. Reg. 51,356, 51,359-60 (1989) (codified at Equal Credit Opportunity Act (Regulation B), 12 C.F.R. § 203.4(a) (10) (2011)) (stating that the HMDA had been amended to require "reporting of data on the race, sex, and income of applicants and borrowers, in addition to the geographic itemization of loans that is currently required").

135 § 12 U.S.C. 2901

136 FFIEC, Community Reinvestment Act, retrieved from https://www.ffiec.gov/cra/default.ht. The Community Reinvestment Act Id. (was created in 1977 to put an end to racial discrimination via redlining but, the effect and stigma attached to certain undesirable neighborhoods had already been created and as a result property values of those homes were on the decline. Today, the overwhelm-

credit needs of all segments of their communities—including in low-to-moderate-income neighborhoods.[137] The CRA extended and clarified the long-standing expectation that banks would serve the convenience and needs of their local communities. The CRA and its implementing regulations required federal financial institution regulators to assess banking institutions' records. This was done in order to ensure banks were fulfilling their obligation to the community; and further, to use these records when evaluating and approving applications for bank acquisitions, mergers, branch openings, and charters. The federal financial institution regulators are: The Office of the Comptroller of the Currency (OCC); the Board of Governors of the Federal Reserve System; and, the Federal Deposit Insurance Corporation (FDIC).

Despite the legislation, the unequal opportunity to acquire homes and home lending continues to plague many minorities. Notwithstanding the nation's attempts through legislation, to repair the damage done by its long history of discrimination, its legacy of inequities continues to thrive as African American and Latinx homeowners—many of whom qualified for standard 30-year fixed mortgages—were marketed subprime loans, which were significant barriers to homeownership and wealth building. Moreover, data shows that *higher income* African Americans were more likely to receive risky loans, compared with similarly qualified white homeowners.[138] Various studies show that much of the reason that these harms continue is due to a few persistent factors:

- A longstanding pattern by lenders and brokers of targeting communities of color for risky, high-cost loans, controlling for other factors such as credit history—with higher income families of color receiving the most unequal treatment.

- Racial discrimination in the terms and conditions of loans by some of the nation's largest banks.

ing number of communities that were redlined during the pre-1968 years continue to be blighted and underserved.)

137 Id

138 See Dima Williams, A Look at Housing Inequality and Racism in the U.S., Forbes, June 3, 2020 retrieved from https://www.forbes.com/sites/dimawilliams/2020/06/03/in-light-of-george-floyd-protests-a-look-at-housing-inequality/#8877c5339ef0

- Unequal maintenance of foreclosed properties, with banks and others disproportionately neglecting properties in communities of color.

- Failure of governmental bodies, including the Departments of Treasury and Housing and Urban Development and the Federal Housing Finance Agency, to adopt or adequately enforce fair housing and lending protections.[139]

d. Effects of Inadequate enforcement

In 2008, a bi-partisan commission released its report on structural impediments to fair housing in federal and state housing programs.[140] Among other things, it found enforcement of the Act was wholly inadequate, that there were a limited number of investigations, Agency and Department records showed deficiencies in inadequate staffing, poor leadership, underutilization of investigative tools, and an imbalance of filed cases despite numerous complaints. These failures can be especially acute in mortgage lending given the significant impact of the mortgage lending industry on property ownership, which is vital to acquiring wealth.[141] Discriminatory practices in the lending industry—such as racially inequitable underwriting, "redlining" minority communities, racially biased property appraisals and predatory lending practices—ensure a persistent gap in homeownership and racial wealth among minorities.[142]

---

139 See generally The Opportunity Agenda, Why Fair Housing, Fair Lending and Equal Opportunity are crucial to solving the home opportunity crisis, publ 2013 retrieved from https://www.opportunityagenda.org/explore/resources-publications/why-fair-housing-fair-lending-and-equal-opportunity

140 National Commission on Fair Housing and Equal Opportunity, Final Commission Report, The Future of Fair Housing, December 2008

141 Felicity Skidmore & Margery Austin Turner, *Mortgage Lending Discrimination: A Review of Existing Evidence*, https://www.urban.org/sites/default/files/publication/66151/309090-Mortgage-Lending-Discrimination.PDF.

142 JOHN YINGER, *Discrimination and Redlining in Mortgage Lending, in* Closed Doors, Opportunities Lost: The Continuing Costs Of Housing Discrimination 63-86 (1995) (discussing important fair lending studies conducted in the early 1990s that strongly suggested persistent racial discrimination in mortgage lending).

e. Limits of Legislation

The Fair Housing Act and its progeny were important legislative steps; but over fifty years later, housing discrimination and residential segregation continue to exist. The 2010 United States Census shows that a majority of white Americans live in neighborhoods that are 75% white, and African Americans live in neighborhoods that are typically 35% white and 45% black.[143]

One of the indirect negative consequences of legislation has been the degrading/devaluation of African American communities. While the traditional forms of red lining and blockbusting were outlawed, they were replaced with reverse red-lining, which targeted minority communities for mortgage loans but at a cost significantly higher than to similarly situated white Americans.[144] Restrictive covenants and deeds are used to indirectly preserve certain neighborhoods, and realtors are showing less options to prospective African-American buyers when compared to white.[145]

According to the Federal Reserve the average median wealth of white households is thirteen times greater than that for the African American household. In 2014, the median wealth for white families in American was $141,900 and only $11,000 for African American families.[146] In 2016, the median white American family had a net worth of $171,000, and the median black family had a net worth of $17,150.[147] Today, the ratio of white family wealth to black family wealth is higher than it was at the beginning of the century.[148] In the fourth quarter of 2020, white households had a total net worth that was over 20 times that of the

---

143 Row, Jess, A Safe Space for Racism https://newrepublic.com/article/138990/safe-space-racism

144 Asma Husain, Reverse Redlining and the Destruction of Minority Wealth. Michigan Journal Race &Wealth. Vol.22. Nov 2, 2016. Retrieved from https://mjrl.org/2016/11/02/reverse-redlining-and-the-destruction-of-minority-wealth/

145 Motoko Rich, Restrictive Covenants Stubbornly Stay on the Books. The New York Times. 15 April 2005. Retrieved from https://www.nytimes.com/2005/04/21/garden/restrictive-covenants-stubbornly-stay-on-the-books.html

146 Joe Valenti & Eliza Schultz, How Predatory Debt Traps Threaten Vulnerable Families https://www.americanprogress.org/issues/economy/reports/2016/10/06/145629/how-predatory-debt-traps-threaten-vulnerable-families/

147 Ingraham, Christopher Racism's Cost for Black Homeowners: $48,000, new study calculates https://www.chicagotribune.com/business/ct-biz-how-racism-destroys-black-wealth-20181128-story.html

148 Sarah Hansen, Here's What the Racial Wealth Gap in American Looks like Today, June 2020, retrieved from https://www.forbes.com/sites/sarahhansen/2020/06/05/heres-what-the-racial-wealth-gap-in-america-looks-like-today/?sh=6e62d33a164c

total wealth held by black households.[149] Racial disparities in wealth are inextricably linked to access to high value homes in high quality neighborhoods, which in turn affect the racial differences in homeownership rates, accumulation of equity, and home value. Homeownership is the main source of wealth for the average American family.[150] Reverse redlining practices effectively increased this disparity under the perverse guise of offering opportunity.

Additionally, there was a shift from direct lending by banks that held their own loans, to the creation of loans by brokers and bankers who then sold those loans to investment firms. Those firms then bundled loans into bonds for sale to investors via securitization. Securitized loans gain profit on short term revenues like points, fees, and origination charges on loans, and their yield spread. This led to minorities being subjected to even more predatory financial exploitation through the increase of securitized loans. African Americans, in particular, went from being denied credit for decades, to being offered numerous opportunities to access credit. The access, however, was predictably sub-prime and other predatory loans that were often the only credit available to them—while whites whom were similarly situated—were able to obtain credit at significantly better terms.[151] These predatory loans were secured by their new American dream homes, and over two-thirds of subprime loans offered were obtained by those who already owned their homes and were refinancing them. By 2006, one of two home purchase loans made to African Americans were high cost, while only one out of every five to white Americans was high-cost.[152] Similarly, for refinance loans made that same year, fifty-two percent of Black refinance borrowers received high-cost loans compared to twenty-six percent of white borrowers[153]. In 2020, homeownership rates show a marked racial gap with 73.7 percent of non-His-

---

149 Juliana Kaplan and Madison Hoff, ...The Racial Wealth Gap has gotten wider over the years, March 24, 2021, retrieved from https://www.businessinsider.com/charts-how-much-wealth-each-race-ethnicity-held-2020-2021-3

150 Chapter 3: Net Worth by Type of Asset. Pew Research Center. 26 July 2011. Retrieved from https://www.pewsocialtrends.org/2011/07/26/chapter-3-net-worth-by-type-of-asset/ also see U.S. Census. America Counts: Story Behind the Numbers. Retrieved from https://www.census.gov/library/stories/2019/08/gaps-in-wealth-americans-by-household-type.html

151 Emily Badger. The Dramatic Racial Bias of Subprime Lending During the Housing Boom. Bloomberg City Labs. 13 Aug 2013. Retrieved from https://www.bloomberg.com/news/articles/2013-08-16/the-dramatic-racial-bias-of-subprime-lending-during-the-housing-boom

152 Been V, Ellen IG, Madar J. The High Cost of Segregation: Exploring Racial Disparities in High-Cost Lending. Fordham Urban Law Journal. 2009; 36:361–93

153 *Id.*

panic whites owning their home. The rate for Asian American, Native Hawaiian and other Pacific Islander households ranked second at 59.1 percent; Hispanic (of any race) was 48.9 percent, and Black householders was lowest at 44.0 percent.[154]

154 U S Census Bureau report, Quarterly Residential Vacancies and Homeownership, First Quarter 2020, Release Number: CB20-58, April 28, 2020

CHAPTER 4
The Ugly (er)

HOW COULD THIS HAPPEN?

Before the Fair Housing Act of 1968, the country's housing policies were severely racialized to the overwhelming disadvantage of African Americans. Many strategies were used to ensure African American dreams of homeownership in communities where they and their families would enjoy equal opportunities would never be realized. Among those strategies, were those that limited mortgage lending and homeowner insurance using redlining.

REDLINING

In 1934 the federal government established the Federal Housing Administration (FHA) as part of President Franklin Delano Roosevelt's New Deal initiative. The purpose of the FHA was to restore the housing market after the Great Depression by incentivizing homeownership and introducing the mortgage lending system still used today. The FHA promulgated policies that provided benefits to white borrowers while denying the same benefits to African American borrowers on the basis of their race and where they lived. The FHA introduced redlining policies in over 200 American cities.[155]

The FHA's 1934 Underwriting Handbook[156] included "residential security maps" used to help the government decide which neighborhoods would qualify

155 Beatrix Lockwood, The History of Redlining, ThoughtCo., retrieved from https://www.thoughtco.com/redlining-definition-4157858

156 Id, reporting that the Home Owner's Loan Coalition (HOLC), which was a federally–funded homeowner refinance program, played a significant role in the Underwriter's Manual

for FHA backing and which should be off-limits. Created in collaboration with the Home Owner's Loan Coalition (HOLC), the maps were color-coded according to these decidedly racial guidelines:

- **Green ("Best"):** Green areas represented in-demand, up-and-coming neighborhoods where "professional men" lived. These neighborhoods were explicitly homogenous, lacking "a single foreigner or Negro."

- **Blue ("Still Desirable"):** These neighborhoods had "reached their peak" but were thought to be stable due to their low risk of "infiltration" by non-white groups.

- **Yellow ("Definitely Declining"):** Most yellow areas bordered black neighborhoods. They were considered risky due to the "threat of infiltration of foreign-born, Negro, or lower grade populations."

- **Red ("Hazardous"):** Red areas were neighborhoods where "infiltration" had already occurred. These neighborhoods, almost all of them populated by Blacks but also included neighborhoods that were primarily Catholics, Jews, and immigrants from Asia and southern Europe residents, were described by the HOLC as having an "undesirable population" and were ineligible for FHA backing.[157]

Redlining promoted racially segregated neighborhoods, disinvestment in black neighborhoods, and reinvestment in white communities.[158] Financial institutions and insurance companies used redlining to identify Black neighborhoods that were then targeted for disinvestment by denying loans, mortgages and insurance coverage, with the effect of devaluing homes and other property within those communities.[159]

---

157 Id. and see Tracy Jan, Redlining was Banned 50 years ago. It's still hurting minorities today., Economic Policy: Analysis, the Washington Post, March 28, 2018, retrieved from https://www.washingtonpost.com/news/wonk/wp/2018/03/28/redlining-was-banned-50-years-ago-its-still-hurting-minorities-today/

158 Will Kenton, Redlining, Investopedia, retrieved from https://www.investopedia.com/terms/r/redlining.asp

159 *Id.*

One example of the extent red-lined mapping effectively marginalized black communities is in Detroit where neighborhoods were graded based on their infrastructure, property values, and most predominantly, the race of the property owners[160]. Typically, white neighborhoods received positive grades of A-B while heavily minority neighborhoods received a D or lower[161]. These neighborhoods were also color coded, and a majority African American neighborhood was color coded red thereby creating the term redlining. As a result, red-lined minority neighborhoods were deemed high risk and received minimal funding from their local and state governments.

Detroit's infamous 8-mile wall was built as a result of red-lining policies. In the 1940s, private real estate developers applied for government funding in order to build family homes for white Americans on an empty plot of land next to a Black neighborhood in a red-lined area, which had received a D grade[162]. The Federal Home Owner's Loan Corporation (HOLC) defined the existing black community as hazardous and based on that finding, the FHA, rejected the developer's application and refused to provide funding to the project because of its proximity to the red-lined 'hazardous' community, in the grade D area. Ultimately, the FHA did fund the project but only after the developer built a 6 feet high wall separating the Black community from the proposed white community.[163] The impact of redlining practices that were finally declared illegal in 1968 is still visible today. Many neighborhoods denied federal benefits in the past and left to deteriorate still remain in decline. Three out of four neighborhoods "red-lined" on government maps more than 80 years ago continue to struggle economically. These communities are generally identifiable by the lack of resources and amenities, outdated infrastructure, fewer job opportunities, and few high-quality educational institutions.[164] Researchers found that nationally, nearly two-thirds of neighborhoods deemed "hazardous" are inhabited by

160 Ta-Nehisi Coates, The Case for Reparations, retrieved from https://www.theatlantic.com/magazine/archive/2014/06/the-case-for-reparations/361631/

161 *Id.*

162 Adams, Michelle, The Unfulfilled Promise of the Fair Housing Act retrieved from https://www.newyorker.com/news/news-desk/the-unfulfilled-promise-of-the-fair-housing-act

163 Gerald Van Dusen, Detroit's Birwood Wall: Hatred and Healing in the West Eight Mile Community, pp 16-17, Publ. The History Press, 2019.

164 Bruce Mitchell and Juan Franco, HOLC "Redlining" Maps: The persistent structure of segregation and economic inequality, a national Community Reinvestment Coalition Report, 2018 retrieved from https://appam.confex.com/appam/2018/webprogram/Paper27686.html

mostly minority residents—typically Black and Latinx. Cities with many such neighborhoods have significantly greater economic inequality. On the flip side, 91 percent of areas classified as "best" in the 1930s remain middle-to-upper-income today, and 85 percent of them are still predominantly white.[165] Moreover, the Federal government's use and endorsement of redlining encouraged similar tactics by private real estate markets. One example is blockbusting.

BLOCKBUSTING

During the period beginning around 1917 and lasting well after World War II, another common practice used to perpetuate racial segregation in residential communities was called blockbusting.[166] Used primarily by private real estate brokers and sellers, the practice created a false market that helped enrich brokers. In order to push white residents out of a neighborhood, realtors used blockbusting to perpetuate the fear of integration by threatening residents that Black families were moving into "their" communities. Out of manufactured fear, whites would flee their homes, which would be sold at above market rates to African American families.[167]

Blockbusting also had the effect of directing whites to suburban areas and leaving the urban communities to minority families, primarily African American. The economic effects on both communities were substantial as the newly African American urban communities were red-lined, limiting any lending and minimizing their values while the suburban communities were 'green-lined' thereby maximizing their values.[168]

165 Id. and supra n. 152

166 See Amber Pariona, What was Blockbusting? describing blockbusting as a way that institutionalized racism revealed itself in suburban America. retrieved from https://www.worldatlas.com/articles/what-was-blockbusting.html

167 Id.

168 Armine Ouazad, Blockbusting: Brokers and the dynamics of segregation, 157 Journal of Economic Theory 811-841, May 2015.

STEERING

Another real estate industry practice that perpetuated residential segregation was steering[169]. Racial steering occurs when a real estate professional guides a minority homebuyer to search for homes only in communities where other minorities live and away from white communities.[170] Mortgage lenders and insurance agents also participated in racial steering by failing to lend or insure properties in minority communities. But it was the real estate sales industry that led the steering practice. The National Association of Real Estate Boards (NAREB) openly promoted steering by stating in its code of ethics up until 1950 that, "a realtor should never be instrumental in introducing into a neighborhood ... members of any race or nationality ... whose presence will clearly be detrimental to property values in that neighborhood."[171] Steering also took the form of restrictive zoning laws that apportioned particular neighborhoods for different racial groups. Blacks and other minorities were prohibited by law from living in certain neighborhoods of several cities, North and South. Zoning laws were the result of government (state) action. So, when the Supreme Court ruled that these policies were unconstitutional, they were then replaced by the racially restrictive covenant which was not the act of government.

RACIAL COVENANTS AND EXCLUSIONARY ZONING

Almost 70 years after the abolition of slavery, local governments were legally enforcing housing segregation through exclusionary zoning laws and city ordinances which prohibited the sale of property to Black people. In 1917, when the Supreme Court ruled zoning laws unconstitutional in *Buchanan v. Warley*[172],

169 Kate Giammarise, Fair Housing is 50, but has its Promise Been Realized, retrieved from https://newsinteractive.post-gazette.com/blog/fair-housing-is-50-but-has-its-promise-been-realized/

170 Racial Real Estate Steering, Sociology Research, retrieved from http://sociology.iresearchnet.com/sociology-of-race/racial-real-estate-steering/

171 Id. and see Art. 34, Code of Ethics, Adopted by the National Association of Real Estate Board at its Seventeenth Annual Convention, June 6, 1924 rev'd June 22, 1928 stating:

"A Realtor should never be instrumental in introducing into a neighborhood a character of property or occupancy, members of any race or nationality, or any individuals whose presence will clearly be detrimental to property values in that neighborhood."

172 245 U.S. 60 (1917)

homeowners swiftly replaced them with racially restrictive covenants; or agreements between property owners that banned the sale of homes to certain racial groups. In 1926, the United States Supreme Court ruled that racially restrictive covenants *between private citizens* constituted legally binding contracts. As a result of the ruling, racially restrictive covenants were widely enacted and used throughout America.[173]

In that case, plaintiffs sought to enjoin a property owner from selling their land to a Black purchaser. The plaintiff argued that in 1921, thirty white persons, including the plaintiff and the defendant Corrigan, owned twenty-five parcels of land, improved by dwelling houses, that they had duly entered into a written agreement which was properly recorded, in which they recited that no part of these properties "should ever be used or occupied by, or sold, leased or given to, any person of the negro race or blood; and that this covenant should run with the land and bind their respective heirs and assigns for twenty-one years from and after its date."[174] The court distinguished the Warley case from the Corrigan case and ruled unanimously that because Corrigan arose from a contract between individuals, the 13th Amendment of the United States Constitution was not implicated. Therefore, any protections derived therefrom had not been triggered. Finding that "individual invasion of individual rights is not the subject-matter of the Amendment," the court concluded that the defendants, including the African American buyer, were not denied any constitutional or statutory right.[175] The ruling opened a floodgate of racially restrictive residential covenants and further greenlit residential segregation practices.

It should be clear that few, if any, truly believed that the Supreme Court's ruling distinguishing private residential covenants from public exclusionary zoning practices, was anything but judicial support of segregation. The FHA Underwriting Manual, 1936 said as much in its article 228 which stated:

173 Corrigan v. Buckley, 271 U.S. 323 (1926)

174 Id.

175 Id. Associate Justice Sanford delivered the opinion of the court. Sanford had served as an assistant attorney general and lead prosecutor in the 1907 case of United States v. Shipp, et.al. where the court exercised original jurisdiction to hear the case against Hamilton County, Tennessee Sheriff Joseph Shipp, who was convicted for allowing a black prisoner who had been condemned to death to by lynched. The case is the only Supreme Court criminal trial in the court's history. He also authored the majority opinion in Gitlow v New York, 268 U.S. 652 (1925) upholding the conviction of a Socialist politician for the publication of a "left wing manifesto".

> "*Deed restrictions are apt to prove more effective than a zoning ordinance in providing protection from adverse influences. Where the same deed restrictions apply over a broad area and where these restrictions relate to types of structures, use to which improvements may be put, and* racial occupancy, a favorable condition is apt to exist. Where adjacent lots or blocks possess altogether different restrictions, especially for type and use of structures and racial occupancy, the effect of such restrictions is minimized and adequate protection cannot be considered to be present. . . . It must be realized that deed restrictions, to be effective, must be enforced. In this respect they are like zoning ordinances. Where there is the possibility of voiding the deed restrictions through inadequate enforcement of their provisions, the restrictions themselves offer little or no protection against adverse influences."[176] [Emphasis added.]

Racial covenants generally took the form of deed restrictions, which required that the property could not be occupied by members of certain ethnic groups. They were promulgated and often instigated by real estate developers, real estate agents and mortgage brokers who would encourage entire neighborhoods to participate. By the time the Supreme Court found racially restrictive covenants themselves unconstitutional in 1947, the practice was so widespread that these agreements were difficult to invalidate and almost impossible to reverse.[177]

While judicial enforcement of racially restrictive covenants was declared unconstitutional in 1948, and the words "race" and "nationality" were eliminated from NAREB's code of ethics in 1950, the practice of steering to ensure racially segregated neighborhoods continued.[178]

DENIAL TO MORTGAGE AND HOME REPAIR LENDING

As if redlining, blockbusting, and racial steering were not enough, significant barriers to housing choice were also created in the financial markets. Many of

---

176 FHA Underwriting Manual, 1936, retrieved from https://www.huduser.gov/portal/publications/Federal-Housing-Administration-Underwriting-Manual.htmlhttps://www.huduser.gov/portal/publications/Federal-Housing-Administration-Underwriting-Manual.html

177 Supra n. 155; [The History of Redlining, ThoughtCo., https://www.thoughtco.com/redlining-definition-4157858]

178 Supra n. 170 [Racial Real Estate Steering http://sociology.iresearchnet.com/sociology-of-race/racial-real-estate-steering/]

these barriers were not only established by federal action, but by local government interventions as well. Rather than leaving the market to its own devices through laissez faire policies as the government had pronounced, the federal government instead took affirmative actions to ensure that African Americans would not share equally in home ownership, mortgage financing, and private lending opportunities.

Before the FHA was created, many homeowners had various types of interest-only, short-term mortgages with balloon payments that often required refinancing. State laws governed lending practices and usually prohibited banks from loaning more than 80 percent of the value of a home for terms typically between five years and 15 years.[179]

Since 1934, the FHA has been responsible for several mortgage insurance programs that were created to boost homeownership. The FHA provides lenders with full loan-loss coverage on mortgages. This coverage allows lenders to recover the full amount of the loan from the FHA in the event a borrower defaults on a loan. The FHA charges borrowers fees to cover the cost of this loan insurance.[180]

In order to provide some consistency in loan terms, in 1936, the Federal Housing Administration published its FHA Underwriting Manual to guide lending practices in home lending. It was the first time that government would play a direct role in easing the burden of home buying in America by presenting various opportunities for potential homebuyers to acquire homes and thereby wealth. But the federal government's assistance would be limited to white homebuyers to the exclusion of African Americans. Some of the racially restrictive underwriting guidelines were:

> "229. The geographical position of a location may afford in certain instances reliable protection against adverse influences. If the location lies in the middle of an area well developed with a uniform type of residential properties, and if the location is away from main arteries which would logically be used for business purposes, probability of a change in type, use, or occupancy of properties at this location is remote. The Valuator should consider carefully the immunity

179 John L. Ligon and Norbert J. Michel, The Federal Housing Administration: What Record of Success?, The Backgrounder, The Heritage Foundation, No. 3006, May 11, 2015 retrieved from http://report.heritage.org/bg3006

180 Id.

or lack of immunity offered to the location because of its geographical position within the city. Natural or artificially established barriers will prove effective in protecting a neighborhood and the locations within it from adverse influences. *Usually the protection against adverse influences afforded by these means include prevention of the infiltration of business and industrial uses, lower-class occupancy, and inharmonious racial groups.*

233. The Valuator should investigate areas surrounding the location to determine whether or not *incompatible racial* and social *groups are present*, to the end that an intelligent prediction may be made regarding the possibility or probability of the location being invaded by such groups. If a neighborhood is to retain stability it is necessary that properties shall continue to be occupied by the same social and racial classes. *A change in social or racial occupancy generally leads to instability and a reduction in values.* The protection offered against adverse changes should be found adequate before a high rating is given to this feature. Once the character of a neighborhood has been established it is usually impossible to induce a higher social class than those already in the neighborhood to purchase and occupy properties in its various locations.

The social class of the parents of children at the school will in many instances have a vital bearing. Thus, although physical surrounds of a neighborhood area may be favorable and conducive to enjoyable, pleasant living in its locations, if the children of people living in such an area are compelled to attend school where the majority or a goodly number of the pupils represent a far lower level of society or an *incompatible racial element*, the neighborhood under consideration will prove far less stable and desirable than if this condition did not exist. In such an instance it might well be that for the payment of a fee children of this area could attend another school with pupils of their same social class. The question for the Valuator to determine is the effect created by the necessity for making this payment upon the occupants of the location. Under any conditions the rating could not be favorable as if the desirable school were available without additional cost. In many instances where a school has earned a prestige through the class of pupils attending, it will be found that such prestige will be a vital element in maintaining the desirability of the entire area comprising the school district."

284 (3). Recorded deed restrictions should strengthen and supplement zoning ordinances and to be really effective should include the provisions listed below. The restrictions should be recorded with the deed and should run for a period of at least twenty years. Recommended restrictions include the following:

- (a) Allocation of definite areas for specific uses such as single or double-family houses, apartments, and business structures.
- (b) The placement of buildings so that they will have adequate light and air with assurance of a space of at least ten feet between buildings.
- (c) Prohibition of the resubdivision of lots.
- (d) Prohibition of the erection of more than one dwelling per lot.
- (e) Control of the design of all buildings through requiring their approval by a qualified committee and by appropriate cost limitations.
- (f) Prohibition of nuisances or undesirable buildings such as stables, pig pens, temporary dwellings, and high fences.
- (g) *Prohibition of the occupancy of properties except by the race for which they were intended.*
- (h) Appropriate provisions for enforcement.

289 (1). Adequacy of Civic, Social, and Commercial Centers.-- These elements of comfortable living usually follow rather than precede development. Those centers serving the city or section in which the development is situated should be readily available to its occupants. *Schools should be appropriate to the needs of the new community and they should not be attended in large numbers by inharmonious racial groups.* Employment centers, preferably diversified in nature, should be at a convenient distance.[181] [all emphases added]

181 Supra n.176 Federal Housing Administration, *Underwriting Manual: Underwriting and Valuation Procedure Under Title II of the National Housing Act With Revisions to April 1, 1936* (Washington, D.C.), Part II, Section 2, Rating of Location

GOVERNMENT SPONSORED ENTERPRISES PROVIDED NO RELIEF FROM WIDESPREAD BIGOTRY

Federal National Mortgage Association (Fannie Mae)

Back before government inserted itself into the mortgage business, borrowers could not count on banks having money to lend where and when the funds were needed. But by the time the Great Depression resulted in high unemployment rates, increased home foreclosures, and severely depressed home values, it was clear that financial interventions were needed to revive the economy. One of the responses to the nation's dire financial straits was the creation of the Federal National Mortgage Association (FNMA). President Franklin Delano Roosevelt signed into law the Act that created FNMA, commonly referred to as 'Fannie Mae' in order to pool together a national fund for mortgage lending to make home ownership affordable to Americans.

Fannie Mae's role was to buy FHA insured loans from lenders, thereby providing liquidity to support the flow of credit. The Housing and Urban Development Act of 1968 subsequently split Fannie Mae into two separate corporations: Fannie Mae, to purchase: (1) conventional (non-U.S. government-insured or government-guaranteed) mortgages that conformed to specific underwriting standards; and, (2) the Government National Mortgage Association (GNMA), or Ginnie Mae, whose full faith and credit guaranty would provide liquidity to lenders while broadening the market for mortgage loan investment beyond portfolio ownership. These loans, insured or guaranteed by the FHA, the U.S. Department of Housing and Urban Development (HUD), Office of Public and Indian Housing (PIH), the U.S. Department of Veterans Affairs (VA) Home Loan Program for Veterans, the U.S. Department of Agriculture's (USDA) Rural Development Housing, and Community Facilities Programs and Rural Development Guaranteed Rural Rental Housing Program (RD) were deployed to encourage Americans to purchase homes.[182]

The Government Sponsored Enterprises that included Fannie Mae (1938), Ginnie Mae (1968), and Freddie Mac (1970), were all designed to ease financial burdens and risks on citizens and financial institutions. Fannie Mae's role expanded after World War II to become the principal federal agency, along with

182 Ginnie Mae, "About Us" retrieved from https://www.ginniemae.gov/about_us/who_we_are/pages/our_history.aspx

the Veteran's Administration, to provide home mortgage insurance. However, none of these financial measures opened the marketplace to African Americans who were consistently denied mortgage loans. Even African American veterans were excluded from participating in the growing wealth of the country they had so valiantly fought for.

GI BILL

The Servicemen's Readjustment Act of 1944 was enacted to ease returning World War II veterans in their transition from active duty to life at home. The benefits of the Act were available to both men and women, but only in rare cases to African Americans. One of the purposes of the Act was to expand the [white] middle class through medical care, higher education funding, and homeownership in suburban communities. Like FNMA and similar programs, the GI Bill housing benefits effectively excluded African Americans because private banks would not make housing loans to them, regardless of their veteran status or of the federal government's support. Moreover, many of the communities being developed were segregated by race using racially restrictive covenants, so that suburbia was closed to African American buyers.

> "Though the bill helped white Americans prosper and accumulate wealth in the postwar years, it didn't deliver on that promise for veterans of color. In fact, the wide disparity in the bill's implementation helped drive growing gaps in wealth, education and civil rights between white and black Americans.
>
> While the GI Bill's language did not specifically exclude African-American veterans from its benefits, it was structured in a way that ultimately shut doors for the 1.2 million black veterans who had bravely served their country during World War II, in segregated ranks."[183]

183 Erin Blakemore, How the GI Bill's Promise Was Denied to a Million Black WWII Veterans, History Stories, History, June 21, 2019, updated September 30, 2019 retrieved from https://www.history.com/news/gi-bill-black-wwii-veterans-benefits

The Ku Klux Klan (KKK) is an American terrorist organization that was established in 1865. It targeted for destruction all Reconstruction-era policies aimed at protecting the rights of newly freed men and women. The organization used fear and terror to discourage African Americans from voting, education, political service and equal housing opportunity, to name a few.[184]

When African Americans became active in politics, winning elections in state and federal offices, the KKK along with other white terrorist organizations, like the Knights of the White Camelia and the White Brotherhood, set out to target all politicians and leaders who endorsed equality. The KKK was able to become a formidable terrorist organization because its members included white lawyers, judges, and law enforcement personnel, as well as wealthy landowners and businesspersons. This allowed lawlessness to go effectively unchallenged. And because its members served in high ranking positions, their presence and influence promulgated inequality wherever the ideals of freedom and equality for targeted minority groups were promoted. African Americans were the group first targeted by the KKK but later targets included Jewish people, immigrants, Catholics, and other people of color.[185]

Throughout the country, and particularly in the south, the KKK used threats, fear, beatings, and lynchings to ensure racial segregation. Among their more consistent struggles has been the fight against integrated residential communities.

In cities across America, Blacks were systematically discriminated against in housing choices and lending because of their race. Banks and mortgage companies failed to grant home loans to African Americans. Federal, state and local governments were actively complicit in housing segregation, employing and supporting Jim Crow practices that included red lining, restrictive covenants, and selective loan grants.[186] Private individuals and associations were likewise complicit in fostering segregation often enforced by American terrorist groups under the watchful and approving eyes of local, state and national governments.

184 See generallyHistory.com editors, Ku Klux Klan, updated April 20, 2021 retrieved from https://www.history.com/topics/reconstruction/ku-klux-klan

185 See Ku Klux Klan, Southern Poverty Law Center retrieved from https://www.splcenter.org/fighting-hate/extremist-files/ideology/ku-klux-klan

186 Coates, Ta-Nehisi, The Case for Reparations, retrieved from https://www.theatlantic.com/magazine/archive/2014/06/the-case-for-reparations/361631/

CHAPTER 5
AMERICAN COURTS' COMPLICITY

American court systems have long been complicit in denying indigenous people and people of color, particularly black people, justice. During the country's early years, U.S. District and Circuit Courts heard numerous matters of admiralty and criminal matters pertaining to the slave trade. These cases often involved proceedings relating to seizure, condemnation, and sale of vessels engaged in the slave trade or criminal cases that pertained to charges of outfitting slave ships and to the service of the masters and crew aboard.[187] The United States Supreme Court heard a number of cases involving slavery in the late 1840s and 1850s. With very few exceptions, slaveowners won every one of these cases as the Court overwhelmingly supported the power of Congress to assist in recovering fugitive slaves.[188]

187 National Archives and Records Administration. American Slavery, Judicial Records, https://www.archives.gov/research/african-americans/slavery-records-judicial.html, court records also consist of papers that relate to fugitive slaves (1851 - 1863), manumission papers (1857 - 1863), papers that pertain to slave's purchase of their freedom, slaves freed by wills, petitions of slaves based on the July 12, 1863 act (12 Stat. 538) that allowed them to file schedules if their owners had neglected to file according to the April 16,1863 act (12 Stat. 376), and emancipation papers based on the April 16, 1863 act. Records that relate to orders to produce a prisoner and show cause for capture and detention. Among these records is a series of papers that relate to fugitive slaves, 1853 -1863, due to the enactment of the Fugitive Slave Act of 1850. The Act allowed claimants to recover fugitives by applying to federal judges and commissioners to establish ownership. Slave owners routinely used writs to reclaim runaway slaves. The records include the actual writs, petitions for writs, return of writs, orders of the Court, and other papers filed in habeas corpus proceedings.

188 Paul Finkelman, States' Rights, Southern Hypocrisy, and the Crisis of the Union, 45 Akron L. Rev. 449; 463 (2011-2012) citing Norris v. Crocker, 54 U.S. (13 How.) 429 (1851). In Norris, the Supreme Court ruled that the adoption of the Fugitive Slave Act of 1850 precluded Plaintiff Norris from initiating a separate actor for a $500 penalty under the 1793 law, marking the case as one of the few victories for the antislavery bar. See William M. Weicke, Slavery and Abolition before the United States Supreme Court, 1820-1860, Journal of American History 65 (June 1978): 34-59.

In 1857, the Court decided Dred Scott v. Sandford, the most notoriously pro-slavery decision in the nation's jurisprudence.[189] Although the case was before the court on the constitutionality of the Missouri Compromise, the court also addressed whether a former slave was considered a "citizen" of the United States. The facts of the case were that in 1785, Dred Scott was born a slave in Virginia. After being purchased by U.S. Army Surgeon, Dr. John Emerson, Scott lived in the free state of Illinois and the free territory of Wisconsin before moving back to the slave state of Missouri. After Emerson's death, the doctor's wife refused to allow Scott to buy his freedom. Scott subsequently filed suit to gain his freedom and that of his wife and family, arguing that residing in free territories mandated their emancipation. Justice Taney wrote the opinion of the court and stated that Scott was not entitled to sue because, as an African American, he was not considered a citizen of the United States. He stated that blacks, either free or slave, had been "regarded as beings of an inferior order", with "no rights which the white man was bound to respect." Taney based his opinion on the legislation and histories of the time when interpreting the Declaration of Independence's statement "that all men are created equal". It was the court's opinion that *the language used in the Declaration of Independence, show that neither the class of persons who had been imported as slaves nor their descendants, whether they had become free or not, were then acknowledged as a part of the people nor intended to be included in the general words used in that memorable instrument...*

Referring to words from the Declaration of Independence, "We hold these truths to be self-evident: that all men are created equal; that they are endowed by their Creator with certain unalienable rights; that among them is life, liberty, and the pursuit of happiness," the Court doubled down on its position that the Negro was recognized only as property when those words were written and adopted adding:

> "The general words above quoted would seem to embrace the whole human family, and if they were used in a similar instrument at this day would be so understood. But it is too clear for dispute that the enslaved African race were not intended to be included, and formed no part of the people who framed and adopted this declaration, for if the language, as understood in that day, would embrace them, the conduct of the distinguished men who framed the Declaration of Independence would have been utterly and flagrantly

189 *Dred Scott v. Sanford*, 60 U.S. 393 (1857)

> inconsistent with the principles they asserted, and instead of the sympathy of mankind to which they so confidently appealed, they would have deserved and received universal rebuke and reprobation."

The majority's opinion is likely rooted in their fervent endorsements of white supremacy beliefs but are not based on fact. Its basis for concluding that African Americans were not people relies on the indefensible notion that the founding fathers were great human beings who would not have permitted slavery if they believed African Americans were people.[190] The court reasoned that if the founding fathers had considered African Americans people yet still allowed slavery then they would be morally corrupt because slavery and the maltreatment that was inherent in it were not the actions of greatness but instead an abomination.[191] Had the court relied on the actual writings of the founders, they would have acknowledged that the principles espoused by these "distinguished" men were so flagrantly inconsistent with morality that the institution of slavery had to be completely destroyed.[192] Instead the court sought to justify the corruption of the men and the institution rather than to find that they both deserved universal rebuke and reprobation."[193]

There is no ambiguity in that the forefathers in their own words recognized the clear fact of the slaves' humanity. For example,

---

190 Id. Speaking for the Court, Taney held that 1) slavery was a specially protected property under the Constitution; 2) free blacks could never be considered citizens of the United States and essentially had no rights under the Constitution; 3) that Congress had no power to ban slavery in the federal territories; 4) no law in the territories could free slaves because that would be an unconstitutional taking under the Fifth Amendment; and 5) that the Missouri Compromise unconstitutionally banned slavery in the federal territories, and by implication the ban on slavery in the Act creating the Oregon Territory was also unconstitutional.

191 Id. Chief Justice Taney, Majority Opinion, stated, "But it is too clear for dispute, that the enslaved African race were not intended to be included, and former no part of the people who framed and adopted this declaration; for is the language, as understood in that day, would embrace them, the conduct of the distinguished men who framed the Declaration of Independence would have been utterly and flagrantly inconsistent with the principles they asserted; and instead of the sympathy of mankind, to which they so confident it appealed, they would deserve and received universal rebuke and reprobation. Yet the men who framed this declaration were great men-high in literacy acquirements-high in their sense of honor, and incapable of asserting principles inconsistent with those on which they were acting." Page 19. https://www.loc.gov/resource/llst.022/?sp=13

192 Robert A. Burt, Dred Scott and Brown v. Board of Education: A Frances Lewis Law Center Colloquium. *What was wrong with Dred Scott, What's right about Brown.* 42 Washington and Lee L. Rev. 1 (1985). Retrieved from https://digitalcommons.law.yale.edu/cgi/viewcontent.cgi?referer=&httpsredir=1&article=1801&context=fss_papers

193 Id

John Jay wrote in 1786, "It is much to be wished that slavery may be abolished. The honour of the States, as well as justice and humanity, in my opinion, loudly call upon them to emancipate these unhappy **people**. To contend for our own liberty, and to deny that blessing to others, involves an inconsistency not to be excused."[194] James Madison wrote, "[W]e must deny the fact, that slaves are considered merely as property, and in no respect whatever as **persons**."[195] And Thomas Jefferson wrote "Nothing is more certainly written in the book of fate than that these **people** are to be free."[196]

That their own words illustrate their hypocrisy in authoring documents heralding freedom (explicit) while holding human beings in bondage (implicit) is a hypocrisy that the court should neither have protected nor sought to justify.[197]

The two dissenting judges faulted the majority for finding that Scott was not a citizen. It was their opinions that the majority had mis-characterized the intent of the founding fathers, noting that blacks were allowed to vote in several states at the time of the Constitution's ratification. According to the dissent, the majority's ruling was "more a matter of taste than of law."[198]

As failed a decision as it was, it flung open the door to judicially sanctioned oppression, establishing the premise that African Americans had no rights that white men were bound to recognize. This would be used to justify slavery and

194 Jay, John, Letter to R. Lushington, March 15, 1786, retrieved from https://classroom.monticello.org/media-item/john-jay-to-r-lushington/ 1

195 Madison, James, Federalist Papers: No. 54 retrieved from http://avalon.law.yale.edu/18th_century/fed54.asp

196 Jefferson, Thomas, Letter to George Washington (1786) retrieved from https://www.nps.gov/thje/learn/photosmultimedia/quotations.htm

197 Anthony Iaccarino, The Founding Fathers and Slavery retrieved fromhttps://www.britannica.com/topic/The-Founding-Fathers-and-Slavery-1269536 stating "In his initial draft of the Declaration of Independence, Thomas Jefferson condemned the injustice of the slave trade and, by implication, slavery, but he also blamed the presence of enslaved Africans in North America on avaricious British colonial policies. Jefferson thus acknowledged that slavery violated the natural rights of the enslaved, while at the same time he absolved Americans of any responsibility for owning slaves themselves. The Continental Congress apparently rejected the tortured logic of this passage by deleting it from the final document, but this decision also signaled the Founders' commitment to subordinating the controversial issue of slavery to the larger goal of securing the unity and independence of the United States. Nevertheless, the Founders, with the exception of those from South Carolina and Georgia, exhibited considerable aversion to slavery during the era of the Articles of Confederation (1781–89) by prohibiting the importation of foreign slaves to individual states and lending their support to a proposal by Jefferson to ban slavery in the Northwest Territory." It must be recalled that these founding fathers, who were/are considered too important to the ideals and character of the nation, were similarly disposed to mistreating Indigenous people and women

198 Supra Note 189

support segregation, which, in 1896, was established as the law of the land in Plessy v. Ferguson.[199]

In *Plessy*, a Louisiana law required the separation of Blacks and whites into racially segregated railway cars.[200] The statute also required officers to assign each passenger according to his race and penalized both a passenger who refused to comply with the statutorily required segregation and any officer, directors, conductors, or employees of the railway who either refused or neglected to enforce the statute. Homer Adolph Plessy was a Louisiana resident of mixed descent, being 1/8th African and 7/8ths Caucasian, who sat in one of the railway cars designated for whites. He was arrested after he refused to move to a railway car designated for blacks. Plessy challenged the statute as a violation of the thirteenth and fourteenth Amendments.[201]

The United States Supreme Court ruled against Plessy and declared that the statute was within constitutional limitations. The court reasoned that the statute was not a violation of the Fourteenth Amendment as it was a proper exercise of the state's police powers, which are usually given great discretion. The court rejected the petitioner's claim that the separation of the races created a state-sanctioned badge of inferiority. The Supreme Court reasoned that while the Fourteenth Amendment's goal was equality, the court did not believe the amendment to be intended to eliminate every distinction such as color. Further the court distinguished social equality from political equality, and found the separate *but equal* accommodations alone did not constitute unlawful discrimination.[202]

---

199 *Supra Note 10*

200 Id. at 551-52.

201 Id. at 442. ("The constitutionality of this act is attacked upon the ground that it conflicts both with the Thirteenth Amendment of the Constitution, abolishing slavery, and the Fourteenth Amendment, which prohibits certain restrictive legislation on the part of the States.")

202 Id, at 551. "We consider the underlying fallacy of the plaintiff's argument to consist in the assumption that the enforced separation of the two races stamps the colored race with a badge of inferiority. If this be so, it is not by reason of anything found in the act, but solely because the colored race chooses to put that construction upon it. The argument necessarily assumes that if, as has been more than once the case, and is not unlikely to be so again, the colored race should become the dominant power in the state legislature, and should enact a law in precisely similar terms, it would thereby relegate the white race to an inferior position. We imagine that the white race, at least, would not acquiesce in this assumption. The argument also assumes that social prejudices may be overcome by legislation, and that equal rights cannot be secured to the negro except by an enforced commingling of the two races. We cannot accept this proposition."

Plessy v. Ferguson is a significant civil rights case in American jurisprudence because it established the constitutionality of state imposed segregation based upon the doctrine of "separate but equal". Separate but equal segregation spread widely across the nation and was legally enforced from 1896 until 1954, when the doctrine fell in *Brown v. Board of Education.*[203] In *Brown*, the Supreme Court held that "separate but equal" facilities were inherently unequal and violated the Equal Protection Clause of the Fourteenth Amendment.[204] Brown specifically dealt with segregation in education,[205] and it would take several more Supreme Court rulings issued into the 1970s before segregation was removed from all laws, including housing laws.[206] Thus, even before Plessy was decided in 1896 to well into the 20th century, the judiciary actively sanctioned government imposed segregation.[207]

With state-imposed segregation having been upheld as constitutional and as a valid use of the states' police powers, various other methods intended to further segregation arose resulting in severe limitations on housing for African Americans. For example, at the private level, race restrictive covenants, which usually prohibited non-whites from buying or occupying residences, were barriers to the spatial mobility of African Americans.[208] At the local level, cities enacted racial zoning ordinances in an effort to control the African American population and the residential expansion of their neighborhoods.[209] At the

---

203 Brown v. Board of Educ., 347 U.S. 483 (1954).

204 Id. at 495.

205 Id. at 483.

206 *Arlington Heights v. Metropolitan Housing Corp.* 429 U.S. 252 (1977) (that proof of a racially discriminatory intent is required in claim that race was a motivating factor in a land zoning decision

207 Roy L. Brooks and Kelly C. Smith, Juridical Subordination, 52 San D L R 825 at 831Some would argue that it continues today with, for example, erosion of voting rights laws, immigration laws etc. but there is no argument that it began well before Plessy asking "Was the Court's complicity in the subversion of racial equality the work of a few rogue justices, a judicial irregularity, or was it an ongoing pattern and practice of judicial decision-making at the highest reaches of our judiciary? There were simply too many cases both predating and postdating the Reconstruction civil rights laws to call the Court's sabotage of racial equality a judicial hiccup. The historical record leads to no other conclusion."; citing Lawrence Goldstone, Inherently Unequal: The Betrayal of Equal Rights by the Supreme Court, 1865-1903, at 12-13 (2011)

208 Supra Note 183

209 Christopher Silver, *The Racial Origins of Zoning in American Cities*, in Urban Planning and the African American Community: In the Shadows 23-42 (June M. Thomas & Marsha Ritzdorf, eds.,1997). Retrieved from .https://www.asu.edu/courses/aph294/total-readings/silver%20--%20racialoriginsof-zoning.pdf

federal level, the Federal Housing Act of 1954 not only enforced and promoted but also furthered residential segregation on a national scale.[210]

ZONING ORDINANCES—STATE ACTION

Zoning ordinances were introduced in the early 1900s as methods to regulate land use and for the planning of cities. Beginning in 1899, Washington D.C. enacted regulations regarding structure height.[211] Zoning regulations revolutionized American land use policy and quickly spread, resulting in increased efforts and intensity to control the cities' land use. Zoning was viewed as a progressive social reform that offered a way to exclude incompatible uses from residential areas but were also seen as a way to slow the spread of slums into better neighborhoods. One by-product of the zoning reform movement was to improve the quality of working class communities by reducing urban congestion.

Los Angeles was the first to enact city-wide zoning ordinances in 1908 triggering a lawsuit opposing the regulation and by 1915 was the first case of its kind to make it to the United States Supreme Court.

The case, *Hadacheck v. Sebastion.*[212] challenged the Los Angeles zoning ordinance as unconstitutional. The zoning ordinance in question proscribed the manufacturing of bricks within the city limits, which included Hadacheck's property.[213] Hadacheck, the owner of a brick manufacturing business who had

210 Massey and Denton 1993 supra note 22 at 51-54; "One of the many ways the government maintained and perpetuated segregation was through the Federal Housing Authority's and Veteran Affairs' race-based loan programs during the 1940s and 1950s, which facilitated the suburbanization of America along racial lines."

211 Supra Note 209

212 Hadacheck v. Sebastian, 239 U.S. 394.

213 Id. Robert H. Thomas. Back to the Future of Land Use Regulation. Property Rights Conference Journal. Vol 7:109. (2018). "But Los Angeles was growing, and in 1909 the Hadacheck property was annexed by the City and became subject to its jurisdiction. The surrounding land—the site of at least one other brickyard—came into the sights of the land speculators and developers. In the mid-aughts, the nearby area was developed as single-family homes. Some of these homes were, and remain today, pretty nice. They were mostly in the arts-and-crafts style. One of these developments—built by "a syndicate of a dozen prominent business men"—was an area they labeled "Victoria Park." That had a nice ring to it, and today the area is still called Victoria Park... The City Council of Los Angeles, over the veto of Mayor George Alexander, used its police powers to adopt an ordinance prohibiting brickyards in certain districts... Remember that "syndicate of a dozen prominent business men" who developed Victoria Park, whose residents were now overwhelmed by the nearby brickyards? One of those "business men" was none other than Josias J. Andrews, who just so happened to be a

operated his business years before the city ordinance, was convicted of a misdemeanor for violating the ordinance. He filed a writ of habeas corpus, and as petitioner he challenged the Los Angeles's city ordinance as a constructive taking under the state's eminent domain power. He further challenged the zoning ordinance as violating the equal protection clause of the United States constitution. The United States Supreme Court upheld the zoning ordinance ruling that it neither constituted taking nor violated the Equal Protection Clause. The Court found that the zoning ordinance did not constitute a taking because Hadacheck retained ownership of the property that was limited only by the activity that he could conduct on his property. As for Hadacheck's Equal Protection challenge, the court reasoned that there was insufficient evidence to establish that the ordinance was an arbitrary exercise of the city's police power, stating "We must accord good faith to the city in the absence of a clear showing to the contrary and an honest exercise of judgment upon the circumstances which induced its action."[214]

When the City of Los Angeles adopted the nation's first citywide zoning use ordinance, its intent was to protect residential areas from industrial nuisances. "What began as a means of improving the blighted physical environment in which people lived and worked...became "a mechanism for protecting property values and excluding the undesirables."[215]

ZONING TURNS RACIAL

Until about 1910, more than 90% of African Americans lived in the south. Beginning around 1917, African Americans migrated from the rural southern states to the urban northeast, Midwest and west, causing cities to experience significant rises in African American population. As African American populations grew and their neighborhoods expanded, cities looked toward zoning ordinances as methods to control and designate where they could live. Baltimore, Maryland, in 1910 enacted the first racial zoning ordinance. Racial zoning

member of the Los Angeles City Council and who chaired the council's Legislative Committee." e

214 Id at 414 and see Village of Euclid, Ohio v Amberly Realty Co, 272 U.S. 365 (1926) where The United States Supreme Court definitively established zoning ordinances as a valid exercise of a city's police power.

215 Supra Note 209f

ordinances worked side by side with de jure segregation to further segregate cities.

Racial zoning ordinances served various purposes. For one, they helped enforce racial segregation. Also, they were effective methods of controlling African American neighborhood growth and development. Racial zoning ordinances ultimately only lasted a short period, from their inception in 1910 until 1917, when the Supreme Court ruled them unconstitutional in *Buchanan v. Warley.*[216]

Buchanan, a white landowner sold a house to Warley, an African American, in Louisville, Kentucky. Louisville's city racial segregation ordinance prohibited blacks from living on a block where the majority of residents were white and eight of the ten houses on the block where Warley was purchasing were occupied by whites. The contract between Buchanan and Warley provided, "It is understood that I am purchasing the above property for the purpose of having erected thereon a house which I propose to make my residence, and it is a distinct part of this agreement that I shall not be required to accept a deed to the above property or to pay for said property unless I have the right under the laws of the State of Kentucky and the City of Louisville to occupy said property as a residence."

The Defendant claimed that Louisville's recently enacted ordinance prevented him from completing the sale since the ordinance prohibited African Americans from moving into mostly white neighborhoods.[217] Because whites were also prohibited from moving into majority African American neighborhoods, the ordinance seemed to impose bilateral and reciprocal obligations to both races, so supporters argued it was race neutral as written and in its application.[218]

Buchanan attacked the ordinance as a violation of the Fourteenth Amendment, and also relied on the U.S. Civil Rights Act of 1866 which stated that "All citizens ... shall have the same right ... as is enjoyed by white citizens to ... purchase, lease, sell, hold, and convey real and personal property."[219] Even

216 Buchanan v. Warley, 245 U.S. 60, 70 (1917). Buchanan v. Warley cites and discusses the constitutionality of a Kentucky statute creating segregated neighborhoods allegedly in an effort to diminish miscegenation and promote the public peace by averting race hostility and conflict. Id. at 70-82.

217 Id.

218 *Id.* at 82.

219 *Id.*

though the United States Supreme Court held the racial zoning ordinance was unconstitutional, the court described its role as having to determine Buchanan's right as a white property owner to alienate his property. The court said, "The question now presented makes it pertinent to enquire into the constitutional right of the white man to sell his property to a colored man, having in view the legal status of the purchaser and occupant." The Court's answer was expressed in terms of the 14th amendment protections, stating"

> *"...[the Fourteenth Amendment] was designed to assure to the colored race the enjoyment of all the civil rights that, under the law, are enjoyed by white persons, and to give to that race the protection of the general government in that enjoyment whenever it should be denied by the States. ... "The case presented does not deal with an attempt to prohibit the amalgamation of the races. The right which the ordinance annulled was the civil right of a white man to dispose of his property if he saw fit to do so to a person of color and of a colored person to make such disposition to a white person."*

The Buchanan court did not find the "right of the black man compelling and in this way largely echoed the sentiment of its prior rulings when it failed to overturn the separate but equal doctrine.[220] The decision did stop passage of racial housing ordinances that segregated neighborhoods by race, however it did not address the question of private action.[221] The actual impact of *Buchanan* as a weapon against segregation is questionable because urban planners used discriminatory planning and zoning schemes into the 1930s in order to continue segregation of the races.[222] *Buchanan* dealt only with legal statutes and racially restrictions by governments that prohibit the purchase, lease, or occupation of property by a particular group of people that were used nationwide to prevent people of color from purchasing homes in predominantly white communities.[223]

220 The Dred Scott court opined that "The framers of the Constitution, he wrote, believed that blacks "had no rights which the white man was bound to respect; and that the negro might justly and lawfully be reduced to slavery for his benefit. He was bought and sold and treated as an ordinary article of merchandise and traffic, whenever profit could be made by it."

221 "Buchanan v. Warley, 245 U.S. 60 (1917)". Encyclopedia of the Supreme Court of the United States. pg 228. Retrieved from http://history.furman.edu/benson/hst321/Buchanan_v_Warley_UShistory-InContext.pdf

222 Supra Note 209

223 Priscilla A. Ocen. The New Racially Restrictive Covenant: Race, Welfare, and the Policing Black Women in Subsidized Housing. 59 UCLA L. Rev. 1540 (2012), 1557. Retrieved from https://www.

PRIVATE HOUSING DISCRIMINATION THROUGH RACIALLY RESTRICTIVE COVENANTS

Racially restrictive covenants were mutual agreements between property owners in a neighborhood that require each party to the agreement not to sell their property to certain races of people. These private covenants were enforced through the cooperation of real estate boards and neighborhood associations. Racially restrictive covenants were popular nationwide as a judicially protected way to prevent people of color from purchasing homes in white communities.[224]

Initially, restrictive covenants met a hostile reception in federal and state courts, either because such overt racial discrimination violated the equal protection guarantees of the Fourteenth Amendment or on the common law property grounds that it violated public policy or constituted an unreasonable restraint on alienation.[225] Yet, the animus dissipated and restrictive covenants became commonplace after the Supreme Court's 1926 decision in *Corrigan v. Buckley*[226] validated their use. The Supreme Court distinguished the Corrigan case from Buchanan, finding that because the Corrigan covenants were private agreements there was no state action involved and thus there could be no Equal Protection violation.[227] The decision had the effect of validating the use of race restrictive covenants as an effective method to control the residential patterns of African American populations. After that decision, land developers, real estate agents, and the Federal Housing Administration all openly embraced segregation and encouraged the use of race restrictive covenants to ensure neighborhoods remained racially identifiable.

The Supreme Court reconsidered its Corrigan decision in 1948 in *Shelley v. Kraemer.*[228] In that case, an African-American family (the Shelleys) moved into

---

uclalawreview.org/pdf/59-6-4.pdf

224 Id. At 1557-1558

225 *Title Guaranty & Trust Co. v. Garrott*, 42 Cal. App. 152, 183 P. 470 (1919) (rejecting the constitutional challenge but upholding the common law one); *see also* Michael Jones-Correa, *The Origins and Diffusion of Racial Restrictive Covenants*, 115 Pol. Sci. Q. 541, 545-47 (2000) (summarizing the results in these state-court decisions).

226 Supra note 173.

227 Id. at 330. 'It is obvious that none of these Amendments [5th, 13th, and 14th] prohibited private individuals from entering into contracts respecting the control and disposition of their own property; and there is no color whatever for the contention that they rendered the indenture void. - Id.

228 *Shelley v. Kraemer.* 334 U.S. 1 (1948).

a neighborhood that was subject to a racially restrictive covenant designed to prevent African-Americans and Asian-Americans from living in the area. Louis Kraemer and other white property owners, brought suit to enforce the covenant in order to prevent the Shelleys from residing in the neighborhood. A unanimous Supreme Court reasoned that while race restrictive covenants were private activities out of the reach of the Fourteenth Amendment, the enforcement of the covenants through the courts constituted state action.[229] Finding state action, race restrictive covenants, if enforced by the courts, would violate the Equal Protection Clause of the Fourteenth Amendment. Thereafter, while private race restrictive covenants were not declared unconstitutional, the agreements were unenforceable by the courts.

LENDING DISCRIMINATION: ANOTHER WAY TO PROMOTE SEGREGATION AND DESTROY WEALTH

Racial covenants were not the only policy used to further racial segregation in America. Another highly effective way of maintaining residential segregation was through lending laws and practices. Even today discriminatory lending practices influences racial residential patterns despite federal law that prohibits creditors from discriminating on the basis of race, religion, sex, familial status, national origin, age, and applicant's use of public assistance.[230] However, in a series of Pulitzer Prize winning articles which appeared in 1988 under the title "The Color of Money," Atlanta Journal Constitution reporter Bill Dedmen described how banks in Atlanta, Georgia discriminated by the racial designation of neighborhoods.[231] His articles illustrated how banks were nearly twice as likely to lend to homeowners and prospective home buyers in low-income white neighborhoods as in affluent black areas.[232] Similar studies have shown

229 Id. at 23. The Supreme Court holding that race restrictive covenants unenforceable and if enforced by the courts would violate the Fourteenth Amendment due to the fact that the courts enforcement would constitute state action in violation of the constitution.

230 Equal Credit Opportunity Act (ECOA), 15 U.S.C. 1691 et seq. retrieved from https://www.justice.gov/crt/equal-credit-opportunity-act-3

231 Bill Dedmen, The Color of Money: Home Mortgage Lending Practices Discriminate Against Blacks., The Atlanta Journal. The Atlanta Constitution May. 1988. Retrieved from http://powerreporting.com/color/color_of_money.pdf

232 Id.

widespread discriminatory lending practices throughout the country.[233] One reason discriminatory practices were so effective is because the Equal Credit Opportunity Act (ECOA) does not entitle a borrower to the credit itself; only to an equal opportunity to credit. Factors such as credit history, expenses, debt, and income determine denial or approval in what appears to be a racially neutral way. However, a recent Berkeley study found that both face-to-face and online lenders rejected a total of 1.3 million creditworthy black and Latino applicants between 2008 and 2015. Researchers said they believe the applicants "would have been accepted had the applicant not been in these minority groups." That's because when they used the income and credit scores of the rejected applications but deleted the race identifiers, the mortgage application was accepted.[234]

TYPES OF LENDING DISCRIMINATION

Federal law recognizes (1) overt discrimination (2) disparate treatment and (3) disparate impact as the three types of lending discrimination under the ECOA and the Act. Overt discrimination exists when a lender openly treats an applicant differently on a prohibited basis. Between 2010 and 2015, D-HUD investigated 173 allegations of overt discrimination.

Overt discrimination occurs when the lender denies a loan or other financing benefit on the basis of a group of people because of their race, religion, national origin, gender, marital status, age or mental capability. Overt racial

233 Robert Bartlett, Adair Morse, Richard Stanton and Nancy Wallace, Consumer-Lending Discrimination in the FinTech Era, Bational Bureau of Economic Research Paper No. 25943, Issued in June 2019 retrieved from http://faculty.haas.berkeley.edu/morse/research/papers/discrim.pdf and see Khristopher J. Brooks, Disparity in home lending costs minorities millions, researchers find, CBS News, Moneywatch, November 15, 2019, retrieved from https://www.cbsnews.com/news/mortgage-discrimination-black-and-latino-paying-millions-more-in-interest-study-shows/; and see David Love, Study: Jason Richardson, Bruce Mitchell and Nicole West, Home Mortgage and Small Business Lending in Baltimore and Surrounding Areas, NCRC, 2015 retrieved from https://ncrc.org/wp-content/uploads/2015/11/ncrc_baltimore_lending_analysis_web.pdf finding that race was consistently the most significant predictor of mortgage lending patterns in Baltimore City and showing that Blacks outnumber whites 2-1 in population but banks grant whites twice the mortgages; and see Lincoln Quillian, John J. Lee and Brandon Honore, Racial Discrimination in the US Housing and Mortgage Lending Markets: A Quantitative Review of Trends, 1976-2016, Race and Social Problems, 12(1); 13-28 (2020); Northwestern University retrieved from https://doi.org/10.1007/s12552-019-09276-x

234 Id. Khristopher J. Brooks

discrimination is typically a blatant stated policy of refusing to lend to a person because of their race. Evidence of overt racial discrimination includes redlining.[235]

Disparate treatment occurs when a lender treats an applicant differently based on one of the protected characteristics (such as race or gender). This type of discrimination can be obvious and blatant, or it can be subtle. Disparate treatment occurs when an applicant who is a member of a denied protected class has substantially the same (or better) underwriting characteristics than an applicant from a group of applicants who were approved by the creditor. In 2017 J P Morgan Chase agreed to a $55 million settlement to resolve a case filed against it by the Department of Justice claiming that Chase charged minority borrowers more than white customers with comparable credit profiles.[236]

Disparate impact occurs when a lender applies a neutral policy to all credit applicants, but the policy disproportionately affects individuals belonging to a certain group based on their race, sex, age, or other protected characteristic. The policy is not intentionally discriminatory, but the policy's effect results in discrimination. In one case, the United States charged that Countrywide's business practice allowed its loan officers and mortgage brokers to subjectively vary a loan's interest rate and other fees from the price it set based on the borrower's objective credit-related factors which resulted in African American and Hispanic borrowers paying more than similarly situated white borrowers. The case settled in favor of the borrowers for $355,000,000.[237]

Targeting African Americans and other minorities for race-based lending has continued since the 1930s and persisted after the Act was passed in 1968.

---

235 Consider Montgomery County, Maryland v Bank of America Corp., 421 F. Supp 3d 170 (USDC, D. Maryland, Southern Division, 2019) and National Urban League b Office of Comptroller of Currency, 78 F.R.D. 543 (USDC, DC, 1978)

236 United States of America v. JP Morgan Chase Bank, NA, 17-cv-347 and See Renae Merle, JP Morgan settles federal mortgage discrimination suit for $55 Million, The Washington Post, Jan 18, 2017 retrieved from https://www.washingtonpost.com/news/business/wp/2017/01/18/justice-department-sues-jpmorgan-chase-for-mortgage-discrimination/ stating that U.S. officials have reached similar settlements with other large banks, including Wells Fargo, for mortgage practices dating to the housing boom and the financial crisis that followed.

237 U.S. v. Countrywide Financial Corporation. 996 F.Supp.2d 247 (2014); and Countrywide home Loans, Inc., No. 2:11-cv-10540-PSG and see Garcia v. Country Wide Financial Corp., not reported in F.Supp 2008 WL 7842104 (USDC, C.D. Calif, 2008) court finding "Hispanic borrower sufficiently stated a claim against lender for disparate impact discrimination under the FHA based on the allegation that the lender offered incentives to its loan originators to charge discretionary, non-risk-based fees in addition to the par rate. Borrower alleged that the practice allowed subjective decision-making resulting in discriminatory impact and alleged that fees assessed in addition to the par rate were not based on market-based factors. Borrower further alleged the impact was significant as he provided statistical evidence of a nationwide disparate impact."

Today, racial discrimination in mortgage lending and communities building continues. At the height of the housing boom in 2006, Black and Hispanic families making more than $200,000 a year were more likely on average to be given a subprime loan than a white family making less than $30,000 a year.[238] The abhorrent practice meant that banks were making loans to African Americans and other borrowers of color often offering them only subprime mortgages with intolerably high repayment rates even though the minority borrower would have qualified for prime mortgage lending.[239]

WELLS FARGO BANK PRACTICES: CASES ON POINT

Wells Fargo Bank was identified as one of the financial industry's big offenders. Wells Fargo's former national top-producing subprime loan officer, a white woman named Beth, told a New York Times reporter about how she and fellow loan officers deliberately targeted minority customers in Baltimore and Maryland suburbs for high-interest subprime mortgages.[240] Beth said that Wells Fargo "saw the black community as fertile ground for subprime mortgages" since working-class minorities were "hungry to be a part of the nation's home-owning mania."[241] Tony Paschal, another loan officer who left Wells Fargo, gave a sworn affidavit that provided detailed accusations of deliberate racial steering into subprime mortgages.[242] This type of predatory lending practice is widely known as "reverse redlining," because rather than denying loans to geographically identified minority applicants, reverse redlining specifically markets their most expensive and onerous loan products to minority customers.[243]

In 2015, Oakland City Attorney Barbara Parker on behalf of the City of Oakland, California filed a lawsuit against Wells Fargo Bank for predatory and

238 Troy McMullen. "The 'heartbreaking' decrease in black homeownership." The Washington Post. 28 Feb 2019. Retrieved from https://www.washingtonpost.com/news/business/wp/2019/02/28/feature/the-heartbreaking-decrease-in-black-homeownership/.

239 Id

240 Michael Powell, *Bank Accused of Pushing Mortgage Deals on Blacks*, THE NEW YORK TIMES, (Jun. 6, 2009) https://www.nytimes.com/2009/06/07/us/07baltimore.html?pagewanted=all&_r=0.

241 Id.

242 Id.

243 Id.

discriminatory business practices[244]. The lawsuit alleged that Wells Fargo targeted minority citizens of Oakland for predatory loans that caused hundreds of foreclosures. Wells Fargo's actions cost the city approximately $50 billion in reduced property values stemming from the foreclosures and their effects on the community. The city alleged that the bank put African American and Hispanic clients in extremely predatory loan products with egregiously pricey interest rates, even though they qualified for much better loan terms. Black and Hispanic borrowers were 2.4-2.5 times more likely to receive predatory loans than white borrowers in the Oakland area with similar credit history[245]. These expensive loans were almost exclusively given to clients in low-income neighborhoods where it would be more difficult for the borrowers to repay the loans causing them to inevitably default[246].

The city also argued that the bank's actions had created racially segregated housing communities in Oakland. They compared it to modern day red-lining that resulted in decreased property values, and ultimately home foreclosures or loss[247]. This in turn would lead to an increase in personal debt, and an inability to relocate into a better neighborhood.

Since 2007, approximately 55 reverse redlining cases were filed against various home financing institution across the country[248]. The most recent one being City of Philadelphia against Wells Fargo Bank[249].

In 2017, the City of Philadelphia filed a lawsuit also against Wells Fargo for Fair Housing Act violations[250]. The lawsuit alleged that Wells Fargo targeted minority borrowers for high-risk and high-interest loans. In their lawsuit, Philadelphia noted that Miami, Florida, Baltimore, Maryland and Memphis, Tennessee were among a list of cities that had brought similar claims against

244 *City of Oakland v. Wells Fargo & Co.*, No. 18-80116 (9th Cir. 2019)

245 Nicholas Iovion, Oakland Says Wells Fargo Cost It Millions Court House News. 23 Sept 2015, https://www.courthousenews.com/oakland-says-wells-fargo-cost-it-millions/

246 Oakland Post. Oakland Files Federal Lawsuit Against Wells Fargo for Predatory Lending, 7 Oct 2015.https://postnewsgroup.com/2015/10/07/oakland-files-federal-lawsuit-against-wells-fargo-for-predatory-lending/

247 Nicholas Iovion, Wells Fargo Rights Oakland's Lending Lawsuit. Court House News. 15 Dec 2017., https://www.courthousenews.com/wells-fargo-fights-oaklands-lending-lawsuit/

248 Albright, Massey, Rugh, & Steil, The Social Structure of Mortgage Discrimination. Hous Stud. 2018. 33(5): 759-776. Retrieved from https://www.ncbi.nlm.nih.gov/pmc/articles/PMC6084476/

249 *Id.*

250 *City of Philadelphia, v. Wells Fargo & Co.*, No. 17-2203 (E.D. Pa. 2018).

Wells Fargo. The city contended that Wells Fargo's discriminatory conduct led to high foreclosure rates in minority neighborhoods. They claimed that between 2004 and 2014, Wells Fargo issued more than 1,000 discriminatory high-risk loans to minorities. Philadelphia found that more than 23% of the loans to minority customers were high risk, while only 7.6% of white customers were given similar terms[251]. These loans were clustered in neighborhoods with high low-income rates, and high African-American and Hispanic populations[252]. Wells Fargo incentivized loan officers to sell riskier loans to people who did not qualify for those loans and charged excessive points and fees[253]. As a result, the loans in these minority communities were nearly five times more likely to result in foreclosure than in predominantly white neighborhoods.

In 2012, the government sued Wells Fargo[254] for engaging in reverse redlining and the bank settled for $175,000,000.[255]

WELLS FARGO NOT ALONE

Primarily because the government sanctioned these discriminatory practices, Wells Fargo was not a lone offender.[256] In fact, it was commonplace and far more widespread than decent people would care to admit. A recent study showed that "a pattern of troubling denials for people of color across the country, including in major metropolitan areas such as Atlanta, Detroit, Philadelphia, Rockford, Ill., St. Louis and San Antonio. African Americans faced the most resistance in

251 J. Weston Phippen, Philadelphia's Lawsuit Against Wells Fargo. The Atlantic. 15 May 2017. https://www.theatlantic.com/news/archive/2017/05/philadelphia-wells-fargo-lawsuit/526758/

252 Max Mitchell, Lending Suit against Wells Fargo Heads to Mediation, 13 Dec 2018 https://www.law.com/thelegalintelligencer/2018/12/13/phila-s-discriminatory-lending-suit-against-wells-fargo-heads-to-mediation/

253 *Id.*

254 *United States of America v Wells Fargo Bank, NA.* 1:12-cv-01150. See complaint at https://www.justice.gov/iso/opa/resources/9512012712113719995136.pdf

255 James O'Toole. "Wells Fargo in $175M discriminatory lending settlement." CNN Money. 12 July 2012. https://money.cnn.com/2012/07/12/real_estate/wells-fargo-lending-settlement/index.htm

256 For example, see: Brentin Mock, Redlining is Alive and Well—and Evolving, Bloomberg CityLab retrieved from https://www.bloomberg.com/news/articles/2015-09-28/eight-recent-cases-that-show-redlining-is-still-alive-and-evolving, and identifying institutions that include Hudson City Savings Bank which served New Jersey, New York and Pennsylvania (settlement: $33 million), Evans bank, which served New York (settlement: $825,000), Associated Bank which served Chicago and Milwaukee (settled for $200 million)

Southern cities - Mobile, Alabama; Greenville, North Carolina; and Gainesville, Florida - and Latinos in Iowa City, Iowa".[257] Banks other than Wells Fargo also settled cases that charged racially discriminatory lending practices including for example, Bank of America's Countrywide Mortgage Company and the PNC bank also settled reverse redlining lawsuits against them for the sums of $335,000,000 and $35,000,000 respectively.[258]

The government policies and the lending institutions' practices were designed to ensure racial segregation continued in spite of the Fair Housing Act.

THE COURTS RESPOND TO GOVERNMENT SANCTIONED SEGREGATION

New York

In *United States v. Yonkers Board of Education*, the court ruled that the City of Yonkers and the Board of Education were intentionally segregative[259]. The plaintiffs claimed that city officials made the preservation of existing patterns of racial segregation a controlling factor in the selection of sites for subsidized housing for residents[260]. The subsidized housing for families was associated mainly with minority residents, so they were typically created in the largely minority occupied areas of the city[261]. Meanwhile the subsidized housing for seniors was associated with non-minority residents and as such were developed in mainly Caucasian neighborhoods. The city's housing history illustrated their complicity in maintaining segregated communities within their boundaries and was a consideration in the court's resolution of the case. The Saw Mill River Parkway

257 Aaron Glantz and Emmanuel Martinez, Modern-day redlining: *How banks block people of color from homeownership*, Chicago Tribune, retrieved from https://www.chicagotribune.com/business/ct-biz-modern-day-redlining-20180215-story.html, 2018

258 United States, Department of Justice. *Justice Department and Consumer Financial Protection Bureau Reach $35 Million Settlement to Resolve Allegations of Lending Discrimination by National City Bank.* 2013. Retrieved from https://www.justice.gov/opa/pr/justice-department-and-consumer-financial-protection-bureau-reach-35-million-settlement

259 *United States v. Yonkers Bd. of Educ.*, 624 F. Supp. 1276 (S.D.N.Y. 1985)

260 *Id.* at 1292

261 *Id.*

was a major dividing geographical landmark that separated the minority lower-income neighborhoods from the mainly Caucasian neighborhoods. Since the mid-1960s, the City placed subsidized housing for families on the Southwest of the Parkway and claimed that their goal was to help rebuild and revitalize the Southwest Yonkers.

When a proposal to build a housing project in East Yonkers was offered, city officials claimed they were worried about the effect a public housing project would have on surrounding property values[262]. The City officials were quoted in the press stating that "*slum-clearance projects* often lead to the eventual deterioration of the surrounding community by the element which they attract," and that the building of an East Side site would be "seriously detrimental to the well-being and interest of area residents[263]." By 1972, the City had constructed about fifteen subsidized housing projects for families and two subsidized housing projects for seniors, and they were all located in the Southwest area of the city[264] minority residents expressed concerns about the oversaturation of low-income housing in the Southwest area. Their fear was that the concentration of low income residents in the area would "lead to the creation and perpetuation of ghettoes"[265]. In 1976, following the creation of the Housing and Community Development Act of 1974, the City Council met and voted against participating in the Section 8 Existing program[266]. Mayor Martinelli, who voted against the program, stated that the City Council was opposed because the program would create geographic mobility for the lower income residents in the city and that certificate holders would be able to go anywhere for housing including predominantly white East Yonkers[267]. Later, the City Council voted to allow Section 8 Existing Certificates but for the exclusive use of senior citizens[268]. The City did not extend the application of Section 8 certificates to families until 1978, and by 1982, only 36 certificates for families were in use, and only 3 of those were in

262 *Id.* at 1298.

263 *Id.*

264 *Id.* at 1313.

265 *Id.* at 1332.

266 *Id.* at 1343.

267 *Id.* at 1344.

268 *Id.* at 1345.

areas outside of Southwest Yonkers[269]. In other words, the City's response to low income housing was to deny low income housing in East Yonkers, except for senior citizen housing in order to appear to be in compliance with the Act and HUD regulations against segregation[270].

The court's review of the historical evidence caused it to conclude that the City did little to encourage the dispersal of housing opportunities for minorities and that the City's methods could not have been more segregative[271]. The court stated that the evidence showed more than 30 years of segregative subsidized housing policy, exhibited by many different groups of City officials illustrating a widespread pattern and practice of discrimination[272]. Despite the years that have passed, there has been a constant theme of racially influenced opposition to subsidized housing in East Yonkers and City officials continue to acquiesce.[273] Ultimately the court opined that but for the chronic and pervasive influence race had on decisions regarding the location of subsidized housing in Yonkers, there would be significantly different results in the City's housing makeup[274].

Maryland

In *Thompson v. United States HUD*, the courts found that the government defendants violated the Fair Housing act by failing to take adequate action to disestablish the patterns of discrimination that had participated in creating racial segregation in Baltimore City, Maryland[275]. The lawsuit was brought by African American residents in Baltimore City public housing units claiming discrimination based on their race. The City had a long history of racial divide and until 1954 there were two functioning sides of the city[276]. The plaintiffs claim that since 1954, the City had still engaged in a pattern of discrimination against African

269 *Id.* at 1346.

270 *Id.*

271 *Id.* at 1353.

272 *Id.* at 1369.

273 *Id.* at 1370

274 *Id.* at 1376.

275 *Thompson v. United States HUD*, 348 F. Supp. 2d 398 (D. Md. 2005), relying on 42 U.S.C.s 3608(e)(5)

276 *Id.* at 408.

Americans with regard to the provision of public housing[277]. The concentration of housing projects in Baltimore City led to a vast increase of African Americans in that city, and a decrease of presence in the rest of the Baltimore region[278]. Between 1940 and 2000, the African American population in Baltimore City rose from 19 percent to 64 percent[279].

In the 1990s, 89% of the public housing units were located in Baltimore City, and those public housing units consisted on average of about 91% African American occupancy[280]. At t he time of the hearing, the racial composition of Baltimore's public housing tenants was over 97% African American, and almost the entirety of the housing projects were located in high-poverty African American neighborhoods[281].

The court found that although officials had a duty to remedy the effects of past discrimination they failed to do so[282]. The court stated that purposeful discrimination of a chronic nature conferred an affirmative duty to remedy past wrongs, and that City officials failed to adequately disestablish the vestiges of discrimination they imposed. The Court found that HUD had failed to consider policies that would have allowed low-income African American families in Baltimore City to be given housing options outside of the racially defined city. The court stated that through the practice of regionalization, which would be the provision of public housing opportunities beyond the boundaries of Baltimore city, HUD had the power and leverage to accomplish desegregation in a way that the local government in Baltimore could not because of jurisdictional limitation[283]. By failing to consider practical regional approaches to fix the effects of racial segregation in the Baltimore Region public housing, the court found that HUD violated the Fair Housing Act and further contributed to the racial disparity in the region.

The Court also found that the Housing Authority of Baltimore City failed to keep accurate records of tenant applications or monitor the placement of

---

277 *Id.*

278 *Id.*

279 *Id.*

280 *Id.* at 461.

281 *Id.* at 467.

282 *Id.* at 443.

283 *Id.* at 462.

tenants, and as a by-product the majority of the African American applicants were housed in Baltimore City[284]. The Court opined that the FHA imposes the duty on HUD to do more than simply refrain from discriminating and from purposely aiding discrimination by others[285]. Action must be taken by HUD to create open, integrated housing patterns and prevent the increase of segregation[286]. The court held that it was inadequate for HUD to try and solve the problem of racial segregation and concentration by simply redistributing the population of Baltimore city within the city limits alone[287].

Texas

The disparate impact standard under the Fair Housing Act applies to both housing provision (the production, sale and rental of housing) and housing credit (i.e., mortgage lending).[288] The disparate impact standard is of critical importance in ensuring that everyone has equal access to housing, regardless of their race, ethnicity, national origin, family status or ability.[289] Disparate-impact claims under the federal Fair Housing Act ("Act") are now a well-established part of housing discrimination law, having been recognized by the lower courts since the 1970s[290] and recently endorsed by the Supreme Court in *Texas Department of Housing & Community Affairs v. Inclusive Communities Project, Inc.*[291]

In 2009, Inclusive Communities Project, Inc., a non-profit housing advocacy organization filed a lawsuit against the Texas Dept. of Housing and Community Affairs (TDHCA), which administers Low Income Housing Tax Credits within Texas. They claimed that the TDHCA granted tax credits to developments located in segregated low-income communities but not in white higher income

284 *Id.* at 450.

285 *Id.* at 457

286 *Id.*

287 *Id.*

288 Fair Housing Act. 42 U.S.C. 3601. Retrieved from https://www.justice.gov/crt/fair-housing-act-2

289 Id

290 See, e.g., United States v. City of Black Jack, 508 F.2d 1179, 1184–85 (8th Cir. 1974).

291 See generally Texas Dep't of Hous. & Cmty. Affairs v. Inclusive Cmtys. Project, Inc., 135 S. Ct. 2507 (2015); see also Robert G. Schwemm, Fair Housing Litigation after Inclusive Communities: What's New and What's Not, 115 Col. L. Review Sidebar 106 (2015) (providing thorough analysis of the decision).

communities thereby maintaining residential segregation in violation of the Act.[292] The decisions in the case during the trial and appellate levels relied on the court's interpretation of the disparate impact theory of recovery and the standards used to apply it. In a divided 5-4 United States Supreme Court decision, the court held that the statutory language of the Fair Housing Act (Act) focuses on the consequences of the actions in question rather than the actor's intent. Disparate-impact liability, it concluded, is consistent with the Act's purpose of preventing discriminatory housing practices because it allows plaintiffs to counteract unconscious prejudices and disguised discrimination that may be harder to uncover than disparate treatment standards. Moreover, the majority found that a successful disparate-impact liability case must make a prima facie case by meeting a robust causality requirement, since evidence of racial disparity on its own is not sufficient.[293]

The Court held that disparate-impact claims are cognizable under the Fair Housing Act upon considering its results-oriented language, and recognized that there was a country-wide failure to reach the Act's central goal of integrating residential communities. Writing for the court, Justice Kennedy opined:

> *Much progress remains to be made in our Nation's continuing struggle against racial isolation. In striving to achieve our "historic commitment to creating an integrated society," ... we must remain wary of policies that reduce homeowners to nothing more than their race. But since the passage of the Fair Housing Act in 1968 and against the backdrop of disparate-impact liability in nearly every jurisdiction, many cities have become more diverse. The FHA must play an important part in avoiding the Kerner Commission's grim prophecy that "[o]ur Nation is moving toward two societies, one black, one white—separate and unequal." Kerner Commission Report 1. The Court acknowledges the Fair Housing Act's continuing role in moving the Nation toward a more integrated society.*

In 2017, the Texas Low Income Housing Information Service (TxLIHIS) challenged a decision by the Houston city council to reverse the city's housing authority's decision to build subsidized housing in a white community near the city's high income Galleria area.[294] The complaint alleged that the city's actions

292 Id. retrieved from https://supreme.justia.com/cases/federal/us/576/13-1371/case.pdf

293 Id

294 John Henneberger. "We demand HUD address City of Houston and housing Authority violations of

were discriminatory on the basis of race or national origin in violation of the Act. The proposed development consisted of 233 affordable housing units to be located at 2640 Fountainview, a white, high-opportunity neighborhood in the city. HUD agreed with the complainants and demanded the City act in conformance with the law after finding that the city's refusal to issue a resolution of no objection to the development was motivated in whole or in part by the race, color, or national origin of the likely tenants. The Department also found that the city's procedures for approving low-income housing tax credit applications were influenced by racially motivated opposition to affordable housing and thereby perpetuated segregation.[295]

TxLIHIS also claimed that the failure of the City of Houston to provide storm water infrastructure and flood plain protections for predominantly minority neighborhoods is discriminatory. It complained that the city's discriminatory history and practices included improperly engineered open storm drainage ditches, locating affordable housing in flood plains and the failure to assure equal flood protection exposes residents of these neighborhoods to repeated displacement during floods, loss of personal property, exposure to mold and environment contaminants, and increased exposure to diseases spread by floodwater. The problems have been raised publicly and repeatedly by TxLIHIS and others with City of Houston officials, and are documented by the City's own study of drainage infrastructure, but have not been remedied by the City.

For more than 100 years, 50 of which followed the enactment of the Fair Housing Act, African Americans and other minorities face persistent discrimination in home ownership, lending and community development. Evolved from overt racism and terrorism, segregation became shrouded in race-neutral policies that were anything but race-neutral. And all the while African American communities continued to decline beneath historically racist design. The executive,

civil rights laws." Texas Houser. 14 Nov 2017. Retrieved from https://texashousers.org/2017/11/14/we-demand-hud-address-city-of-houston-and-housing-authority-violations-of-civil-rights-laws/. Also see TLIHIS letter to HUD regarding challenges to the civil rights certification of the City of Houston and the Houston Housing Authority retrieved from https://www.dropbox.com/s/plb-9fzfkyz1ioq7/2017.10.31%20M.%20Allen%20ltr%20to%20N.%20Rackleff%2C%20D.%20Blom%2C%20A.%20Farias.pdf?dl=0

295 Id. HUD letter retrieved from https://www.dropbox.com/s/plb9fzfkyz1ioq7/2017.10.31%20M.%20Allen%20ltr%20to%20N.%20Rackleff%2C%20D.%20Blom%2C%20A.%20Farias.pdf?dl=0 Also see. HPM News Staff. "Breaking: HUD Says Houston Broke Law Nixing Affordable Housing Complex." Houston Public Media. 13 Jan 2017 https://www.houstonpublicmedia.org/articles/news/2017/01/13/183650/breaking-hud-says-houston-broke-law-nixing-affordable-housing-complex/

legislative and judicial branches of government have weighed in with promises, commitments, laws and policies for change and yet discrimination continues and in some cases, even worse today than it was more than 50 years ago.[296] Not to ignore the strides that have been made facially, the undeniable truth is that the gaps between black wealth, income, homeownership, education and more have remained static or has broadened. The intentional discriminatory policies and practices played significant roles in creating and maintaining communities of opportunity that are white, and communities lacking opportunity that are decidedly minority. Going forward all communities, not just white or wealthy ones, should be developed and maintained as communities of opportunity.

---

296 See Jake Horton, George Floyd: How far have African Americans come since the 1960s? May 2021, retrieved from https://www.bbc.com/news/world-us-canada-52992795; and see Heather Long and Andrew Van Dam, The black-white economic divide is as wide as it was in 1968, retrieved from https://www.washingtonpost.com/business/2020/06/04/economic-divide-black-households/, and see Janelle Jones, John Schmitt and Valerie Wilson, 50 Years after the Kerner Commission, February 2018 retrieved from https://www.epi.org/publication/50-years-after-the-kerner-commission/, and see Sharon Austin, The Conversation: How black Americans' lives have- and haven't- changed since Dr. King's death, retrieved from https://www.pbs.org/newshour/nation/how-black-americans-lives-have-and-havent-changed-since-dr-kings-death; and see Gwynn Guilford, Black income is half that of white households in the US—just like it was in the 1950s, September 2018 retrieved from https://qz.com/1368251/black-income-is-half-that-of-white-households-just-like-it-was-in-the-1950s/

CHAPTER 6
After the Act: Promises Broken

Numerous promises made to America's former slaves were broken. Dr. Henry Louis Gates, Jr. challenges us to consider "how profoundly different race relations in the United States would be if America had implemented and enforced only one of its promises to former slaves: the promise of '40 acres and a mule'."[297] "Had the former slaves actually had access to the ownership of land, of property; if they had had a chance to be self-sufficient economically, to build, accrue and pass on wealth", he continues, "but it was a promise not to be realized for the overwhelming majority of the nation's former slaves, who numbered about 3.9 million."[298] An interesting corollary to America's failure to compensate former slaves after the emancipation is that it did enact a reparations program that paid,

297 Henry Louis Gates, Jr., the Truth behind the '40 Acres and a Mule', retrieved from https://www.pbs.org/wnet/african-americans-many-rivers-to-cross/history/the-truth-behind-40-acres-and-a-mule/

298 Id. Describing how this promise was secured by "Special Field Order No. 15 and approved by President Abraham Lincoln. The response to the Order was immediate. An editorial note intoned that "From this it will be seen that the colored people down South are not so dumb as many suppose them to be," reflecting North-South, slave-free black class tensions that continued well into the modern civil rights movement. The effect throughout the South was electric: As Eric Foner explains, "the freedmen hastened to take advantage of the Order." Baptist minister Ulysses L. Houston, one of the group that had met with Sherman, led 1,000 blacks to Skidaway Island, Ga., where they established a self-governing community with Houston as the "black governor." And by June, "40,000 freedmen had been settled on 400,000 acres of 'Sherman Land.'" "And what happened to this astonishingly visionary program, which would have fundamentally altered the course of American race relations? Andrew Johnson, Lincoln's successor and a sympathizer with the South, overturned the Order in the fall of 1865, and, as Barton Myers sadly concludes, "returned the land along the South Carolina, Georgia and Florida coasts to the planters who had originally owned it" – to the very people who had declared war on the United States of America." Citing Barton Myers, Sherman's Field Order no. 15 retrieved from https://www.georgiaencyclopedia.org/articles/history-archaeology/shermans-field-order-no-15, last edited 9.29.2020 and further citing Eric Foner, Reconstruction: America's Unfinished Revolution, 1863-1877

in 2020 equivalent dollars, $23 million in Treasury Department Funds to white slaveholders.[299]

Another promise that if honored could have strongly impacted the lives of former slaves and their descendants is the promise of the 14th amendment to the US Constitution.

> "The amendment's ratification on July 9, 1868, shortly after African-Americans were emancipated from slavery, represented a turning point in the country's history. Its passage was an effort to provide substance to the Declaration of Independence's promises of freedom and equality, which from the beginning had not applied to significant parts of the population, including Black people and women. And though those promises were continually reneged upon, the 14th Amendment remained a source of aspiration and hope.
>
> Although the 14th Amendment is frequently invoked now, particularly by conservative judges and commentators, to attack affirmative action and efforts to desegregate schools under the guise of "colorblindness," the Fourteenth Amendment was never a colorblind document. The amendment was enacted specifically for purposes of assisting newly freed Black people. Although the 13th Amendment ended slavery, it left uncertain the status of those who had been kept in bondage.[300]

Freedom dues were promised to black and white indentured servants in colonial America. These dues were a measure of payment for the servants' work but were often unpaid in land especially to African servants.[301]

The Fair Housing Act of 1968 was essentially enacted to rid the American housing industry of its long history of racial discrimination. Questions persist: Why after more than fifty years later, does housing discrimination and residential segregation continue to exist. Why do latest Census show that a majority of

---

299 Kali Holloway, Since Emancipation, the United States has Refused to Make Reparations for Slavery, March 2020 retrieved from https://www.thenation.com/article/society/slavery-reparations-compensated-emancipation-act/

300 See Dennis Parker, The 14th Amendment was Intended to Achieve Racial Justice—And we Must keep it that way, July 9, 2018, https://www.aclu.org/blog/racial-justice/race-and-inequality-education/14th-amendment-was-intended-achieve-racial-justice

301 Evan Kleiman and Natalie Baszile, Explaining the broken promises of 'freedom dues', June 25, 2021 retrieved from https://www.kcrw.com/culture/shows/good-food/we-are-each-others-harvest-black-farming-legacy-land/clyde-ford-americas-broken-promises-african-american-farmers

white Americans live in neighborhoods that are seventy-five percent white, and African Americans live in neighborhoods that are typically thirty-five percent white, and forty-five percent Black. [302] In part, the answers lie both in the intentional segregation before the Act and in the unintentional consequences of the Act itself which gave rise to indirect, negative actions that degraded and devalued African American communities including characterizing them as 'communities without opportunity.

Following every legislative effort to curb residential segregation, financial institutions, local, state and federal governments, individuals and private communities averted the new laws by using alternative means like reverse redlining, deed restrictions and policies and practices that include discriminatory actions by real estate appraisers and realtors who continue to show fewer options to prospective buyers who are African American than to white prospects. The impact on wealth is palpable. Racial disparities in wealth are inextricably linked to access to high value homes in high quality neighborhoods.[303] In turn, this access has a detrimental effect on racial differences in homeownership rates, accumulation or equity, home value, these are the main sources of wealth for the average American family.[304]

Public policies consistently play a central role in establishing and enforcing patterns of racial segregation in American neighborhoods, alongside discriminatory practices by private-sector institutions and individuals. Yet, no single causal process can explain the persistence of residential segregation in America today. Discrimination, information gaps, stereotypes, fears, and disparities in purchasing power all work together to perpetuate segregation, even though many Americans—minority and white—say they want to live in more diverse neighborhoods. Public policies must intervene to break the cycle of residential segregation. But, because the causes of segregation are interconnected, no single

302 Row, Jess, A Safe Space for Racism https://newrepublic.com/article/138990/safe-space-racism

303 See Homeownership: A Key to Wealth-Building, retrieved from https://frederickrealestateonline.com/home-ownership-key-to-wealth-building/ citing Harriet Torry, US Household Net Worth rose by $2.07 trillion in 3rd Quarter, The Wall Street Journal, December 6, 2018 reporting that a typical homeowner's net worth was $241,400, while that of renters was between $5,200 and $5,500 in 2013 retrieved from https://www.wsj.com/articles/u-s-household-net-worth-rose-by-2-070-trillion-in-3rd-quarter-1544115583

304 William Darity, Jr., Darrick Hamilton, Mark Paul, Alan Aja, Anne Price, Antonio Moore, and Caterina Chiopris, What We Get Wrong with Closing the Racial Wealth Gap, Samuel DuBois Cook Center on Social Equity, Duke University, April 2018 retrieved from https://socialequity.duke.edu/wp-content/uploads/2020/01/what-we-get-wrong.pdf

intervention can succeed on its own. Instead, multidimensional strategies are needed to simultaneously tackle the multiple causes of segregation. Sustainable communities cannot be achieved as long as the current levels of neighborhood segregation, exclusion, and inequality persist. Nor can it occur under the burden of racially stereotypical underpinnings that one community provides opportunity while the other does not.

Although fair lending claims will, for the most part, continue to focus on disparate treatment recovery, disparate impact should not be ignored, and a compliance program should be in tune with these acknowledgments. But it is not the legal debate over the value of disparate impact that poses the greatest threat to fair housing in America, but federal policies like those promulgated between 2017 and 2021.[305] Anti-Fair Housing policies during those years strengthens the foundation for breaking the biggest promise of all...equality.[306]

---

305 Stephen M. Dane, Fair Housing Policy under the Trump Administration, American Bar Association November 30, 2019 retrieved from https://www.americanbar.org/groups/crsj/publications/human_rights_magazine_home/economic-justice/fair-housing-policy-under-the-trump-administration/ and see Tim Nelson, The Trump Administration's Highly-Politicized Roll Back of Obama-Era Fair Housing Rule Raises Concerns, July 30, 2020 retrieved from https://www.architecturaldigest.com/story/trump-hud-fair-housing-act, also see Izzy Woodruff, Trump Administration Guts Fair Housing Protections, retrieved from https://nationalfairhousing.org/2020/09/24/trump-administration-guts-fair-housing-protections/

306 See generally, Gregory D. Squires, Trump's attempt to weaken fair housing rules is beyond tone deaf, July 20, 2020 retrieved from American Banker, https://www.americanbanker.com/opinion/trumps-attempt-to-weaken-fair-housing-rules-beyond-tone-deaf; and see Pro Publica, Revealed: Trump regulator quietly shelved discrimination investigations into Bank of America and other Banks, July 12, 2020 retrieved from https://www.rawstory.com/2020/07/revealed-trump-regulator-quietly-shelved-discrimination-investigations-into-bank-of-america-and-other-banks/; and Patrick Sisson, How Trump is rolling back housing desegregation rules, explained, Curbed, Jan 28, 2020 retrieved from https://www.curbed.com/2020/1/28/21101127/trump-hud-housing-segregation-ben-carson

CHAPTER 7
The Sins of the Fathers

Even among well-meaning Americans there is an underlying question of why white people today should be held responsible for the sins of their ancestral fathers.[307] But there is no need to look further than today's laws, policies and practices to determine that they continue to treat African Americans differently, disparately and to their detriment based on race. Much has been written about the last two decades of America's crime policies and laws that vividly portray the effects of current racism that is systemic in our country.[308] The war against drugs, overcriminalization, mass incarceration, denial of bail, and racial profiling barely pierce the surface of criminal injustice systems that have plagued African Americans from the days from fugitive slave laws to now.[309] Throughout this same period African Americans have been systematically denied equal opportunities to participate in business development, particularly in government contracting,[310] equal employment opportunities[311] and in equal pay.[312]

307 Kim Forde-Mazuri. Taking Conservatives Seriously: A Moral Justification for Affirmative Action and Reparations. Cal Law Review. Vol 92 No 3. May 2004. Retrieved from https://www.jstor.org/stable/3481453?seq=1

308 Report to the United Nations on Racial Disparities in the U.S. Criminal Justice System. The Sentencing Project. 19 April 2018. Retrieved from https://www.sentencingproject.org/publications/un-report-on-racial-disparities/

309 Id

310 Danyelle Solomon, Connor Maxwell, and Castro August, Systematic Inequality and Economic Opportunity. Center for American Progress. 7 Aug 2019. Retrieved from https://www.americanprogress.org/issues/race/reports/2019/08/07/472910/systematic-inequality-economic-opportunity/

311 Id

312 Id

Startling disparities in housing and housing financing have systematically affected African Americans in areas that include housing choice, wealth accumulation, homeownership, housing costs, and insurance, to name a few, during the last few decades. Actions that though rooted in historical behaviors, remain constant and are deployed to this day. So, while there may be debate over whether the sons (and daughters) bear responsibility for their fathers' (and mothers') systems of inequality, there should be no question but that the sons and daughters must bear responsibility for creating and maintaining their own systems of inequality. Even if those actions are not intentional, the evidence of these systems is clear. "The only thing necessary for the triumph of evil is for good men to do nothing."[313]

WAGE GAPS

A persistent gap in wages exists among American workers based on race and gender.[314] Internationally, America particularly exhibits high levels of income inequality, with estimates of 70% of the world's countries being more equal than the United States.[315]

313 Edward Burke, British philosopher and statesman who lived in the 1700s. Quote retrieved from https://www.azquotes.com/author/2186-Edmund_Burke

314 Eileen Patten, Racial, gender wage gaps persist in U.S. despite some progress, Fact Tank July 1, 2016 retrieved from https://www.pewresearch.org/fact-tank/2016/07/01/racial-gender-wage-gaps-persist-in-u-s-despite-some-progress/

315 Amber Pariona, Average Income by Race and Gender-USA, July 2019, retrieved from https://www.worldatlas.com/articles/income-inequality-by-race-and-gender-in-the-u-s.html#:~:text=Income%20Inequality%20By%20Race%20And%20Gender%20In%20The,%20%20%24734%2Fweek%20%208%20more%20rows%20

INCOME INEQUALITY BY RACE AND GENDER IN THE U.S.

Rank	Ethnicity And Gender	Weekly Wages
1	Asian Males	$1,080/week
2	White Males	$897/week
3	Asian Females	$841/week
4	White Females	$734/week
5	Black Males	$680/week
6	Native Hawaiian & Pacific Islander Males	$632/week
7	Native American & Alaskan Males	$623/week
8	Hispanic Males	$616/week
9	Black Females	$611/week
10	Native Hawaiian & Pacific Islander Females	$556/week
11	Hispanic Females	$548/week
12	Native American & Alaskan Females	$529/week

316

A recent study of the wage gap in America, found that over the majority of the last 50 years, African Americans have experienced recessionary-level unemployment rates and widespread residential segregation.[317] Further, despite everything that has changed over the past 56 years, substantial discriminatory earning gaps among various population sectors persist. The largest wage gap by far is by race.[318]

Apparently, this gap is trending against equality. Black workers "have been losing ground since 2000, with larger [B]lack-white wage gaps across the entire distribution of earnings." For example, Black wages at the median in 2019 were only 75.6 percent of white wages, a 3.6 percent increase from 2000, when Black wages at the median were 79.2 percent of white wages. Even when looking at wages by education level, Blacks are paid less than whites. Blacks with advanced

316 Id.

317 Ward Williams, Wage Gaps by Race, August 2020 retrieved from https://www.investopedia.com/wage-gaps-by-race-5073258

318 Id.

degrees are paid 82.4 cents for each dollar earned by whites with an advanced degree.[319]

On average, white workers are paid more than black and Hispanic workers at nearly every education level

Average hourly wages, by race/ethnicity and education, 2019

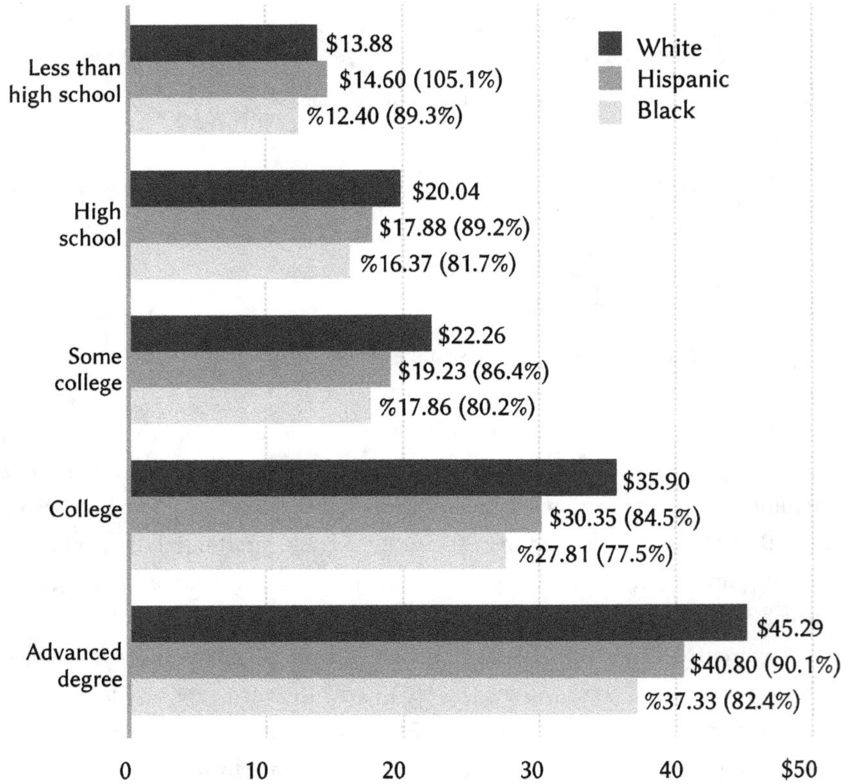

Chart Data

Source: Author's analysis of EPI Current Population Survey Extracts, Version 1.0 (2020). https://microdata.epi.org

Economic Policy Institute

319 Shazar Ziv, Salary History bans reduce racial and gender wage gaps; every CEO should use them, Jun 2020, retrieved from https://www.forbes.com/sites/shaharziv/2020/06/23/salary-history-bans-reduce-racial-and-gender-wage-gaps-implement-them-nationwide/?sh=14394747151c

Wealth provides families the means to invest in their children's education, to start a business, relocate for new and better opportunities, buy a house, and have greater participation in the democratic process. Many households in Black communities cannot afford to pay for reliable internet or electronic devices to facilitate remote learning. White workers have been more likely to work remotely during the COVID -19 pandemic and have resources to devote to their children's remote learning environment, while Black workers are more likely to still be going to work in person. The pandemic has created the perfect storm of factors that [could] drive wealth for African Americans and white households even further apart.[320] The importance of wealth and its impacts are difficult to overstate as it affects every major area of American life including educational attainment and performance,[321]health outcomes,[322]homeownership,[323]democratic engagement,[324]to name a few. When wealth is systematically denied to people because of their race or ethnicity or gender or other impermissible reason we should examine why the gap exists and how to close it.[325]

LIES, DENIALS AND ALTERNATIVE REALITIES

American housing policy and practices continue to be rooted on the false premises used to support the lie of white supremacy. This baseless foundation is used to support social structures that value and devalue lives based on race. Onto

320 Christian E. Weller and Lily Roberts, Eliminating the Black-White Wealth Gap is a Generational Challenge, March 19, 2021, Center for American Progress retrieved from https://www.americanprogress.org/issues/economy/reports/2021/03/19/497377/eliminating-black-white-wealth-gap-generational-challenge/

321 Amy J. Orr, "Black-White Differences in Achievement: The Importance of Wealth." Sociology of Education, vol. 76, no. 4, 2003, pp. 281–304. retrieved from JSTOR, www.jstor.org/stable/1519867.

322 Torrance T. Stephens. "Conceptualizing Racial and Ethnic Disparities in Health in the Form of Intergenerational Transfer of Wealth." Phylon (1960), vol. 50, no. 1/2, 2002, pp. 161–165. JSTOR, retrieved from www.jstor.org/stable/4150007.

323 Laurie S. Goodman, and Christopher Mayer. "Homeownership and the American Dream." The Journal of Economic Perspectives, vol. 32, no. 1, 2018, pp. 31–58. JSTOR, retrieved from www.jstor.org/stable/26297968.

324 Jedediah Purdy, Wealth and Democracy, Vol. 58, Wealth (2017) pp 235-260, JSTOR retrieved from www.jstor.org/stable/26785954

325 Vanessa Williamson, Closing the racial wealth gap requires heavy, progressive taxation of wealth, Brookings, December 2020 retrieved from https://www.brookings.edu/research/closing-the-racial-wealth-gap-requires-heavy-progressive-taxation-of-wealth/

these structures we grant unfair benefits to some while denying these same benefits to others. These lies based on a lie based on another lie ultimately create a sustained and alternate reality. To establish a fair open system that exposes the lies and rejects the denials, we must commit ourselves and resources to destroying the foundations on which they rest.

White supremacy is the fallacy that white people are, by virtue of their race, superior to all other races and as such are entitled to reign supreme in authority, power, status and wealth. It is a political and social system designed and constructed to ensure that all non-whites are never treated equally to whites but instead will be forever dominated by the privileged white class. This ideology, predicated on lies, is strongly endorsed explicitly and implicitly and will take more than a passing effort to deconstruct and eliminate. Overthrowing the ideology calls for exposing the lies and requiring all systems transformations.

During America's early years, an organization called the American Colonization Society developed the African Repository and Colonial Journal. The primary purpose of the group was to return freed Africans back to Africa to an area that ultimately became known as Liberia. This organization was comprised of leaders of religious, political and social groups and held its annual meetings in the United States supreme court building.

Lie 1: African Contributions to the World Society

The early history of the "Negro race" as presented by the learned men of the American Colonization Society is recounted in Volume 1 of the African Repository.[326]

> "To those who are at all acquainted with the early history of mankind, it must afford a curious commentary upon the mutability of human affairs, to hear the strange conjectures which are sometimes indulged about the origin of the Negro race. In defiance of all our records of antiquity, both sacred and profane—they are contemptuously spoken of as a distinct order of beings; the connecting link between men and monkies.

326 African Repository and Colonial Journal, Vol I., publ. by Order of the Managers of the American Colonization Society, Washington City 1826; Klaus Reprint Corp 1967 at 17-22 on file at the Harvard University Library retrieved from https://babel.hathitrust.org/cgi/pt?id=hvd.32044010429827&view=1up&seq=5&size=125

Those who talk in this way, do not recollect, or perhaps do not know, that the people whom they traduce, were for more than a thousand years (that is ten times as long as this Government has been in existence,) the most enlightened on the globe.

They were called Ethiopians, from two Greek words [meaning burnt and skin] denoting the colour of their skins; and the spirit of adventure by which they were distinguished, together with the superiority which they every where manifested over the nations among whom they dwelt, rendered this name illustrious throughout Europe, Asia and Africa. ...

The ...Ethiopians established the first government, and the first regular policy, which history records. The first great city which we have described in history was built by them....Diodorus [Siculus] says "never did any city come up to the greatness and magnificence of this"[327] All those mounds and causeways, (says a modern writer of ability) the high roads and stately structures which have been attributed to Semiramis of Babylonia, are the works of these people."

Thus at a time when the rest of the world was in a state of barbarism, the Ethiopian family were exhibiting prodigies of human genius, at which mankind have not yet ceased to wonder—and which they have never so much as dreampt of being able to transcend....

They subjugated the whole of Upper Egypt, which they held in bondage for more than three hundred years. They found that country in a state of barbarism; they left it the mother of science, and the mistress of the world! ...They colonized lower Egypt, which was before scarcely habitable....

And the same daring spirit...built a city upon the ruins of the Tower of Babel; as if in mere mockery of men, threw up pyramids, obelisks, and mausolea, which even now baffle conjecture...

And there can be no doubt that the vast region from which our slaves are brought, was first settled by this hardy and adventurous population. Of this there are many proofs, -1st the striking accordance of complexion, language,

327 Id. citing Diod. Lib. 2. P. 90; 98)

manners, customs, etc, by which (with slight shades of variety,) the inhabitants of the south and west are assimilated to those whom we know to be of Ethiopian extraction. 2d, The whole southern peninsula of African was once called Ethiopia.—3d,...there is a tradition handed down from time immemorial in that country, that Cush was their father, and actually dwelt among them—4th, It is expressly related by historians that the Cushites, "traversed a great part of Africa"...lastly, the geographical situation of the country, renders it almost a matter of demonstration....

This people...were rewarded for their wisdom. Wherever they went they were in every respect superior to the natives. ...If any should hesitate to adopt the account which has been given of the Cushites or Ethiopians, and thence take occasion to controvert the doctrine of the benefits derived from the Negro race, he might be told that the Egyptians themselves were Negroes. A single quotation from Herodotus "the father of history", will be sufficient for this point....I believe...a colony of Egyptians, because like them they have black skins and frizzled hair."

How are we astonished, proclaims Volney [French Nobleman Constantin François de Chasseboeuf, comte de Volney], when we reflect that to the race of Negroes, at present our slaves, and the objects of our extreme contempt, we owe our arts, sciences, and even the very use of speech...."[328]

Lie 2: Race dictates physiological and intellectual differences

Until the 18th century, "race" had a generalized meaning akin to "type, sort or kind".[329] By the 18th century, race became used as a ranking of the peoples in the English colonies—with Europeans referred to as free people, indigenous Americans referred to as Amerindians and black slaves who were Africans.[330]

328 Id. relying for support the following: Dr. Griffin's Plea for Africa, Rees' Cyclopoedia, Articles, "Cush, Aurite, Dispensation of Mankind, Egypt, Shepherds, Ethiopia, Copti, Carthage, Sokman, &c. Bryant's Observations on Ancient History, Calmet's Dic. Of Rib, under Cush, Cathan, ...Brown's Dictionary of the Bible, "Cush", Gregoire on the Literature of Negroes, Clarkson on Slavery, Well's Geography, vol. 1 p. 100, Bibliothica of Ravanelles, "Cush," Strabo's Geography, p21, 24.

329 The history of the idea of race, Britannica retrieved from https://www.britannica.com/topic/race-human/The-scientific-debate-over-race

330 Id.

This process of separating people was historical for the English who had long separated themselves from others. For example, the Irish were thought of as "others" or "savages" incapable of being civilized. When the English sought to use the Irish as forced labor, the Irish resistance blocked the effort, forcing the English to look elsewhere. They set their sights on colonizing America where they forcibly attacked and effectively enslaved indigenous people before enslaving Africans, who, by the 1690s were formally separated from the Europeans, who were categorized as white and creating a system of permanent slavery of Africans. American legislative bodies began legislating racial categorization and contempt by whites against blacks.

While the idea of permanent slavery troubled many, Christianity provided the rationalization for slavery by defaming Africans as heathens and laying the groundwork for dehumanizing Africans. It is instructive that the reasons for preferring Africans as slaves to the indigenous people was principally that the Africans were sophisticated cultivators who knew how to grow food and crops in tropical soils. "In this, they surpassed the Irish who had been enslaved on plantations in the Caribbean; with no tradition of agriculture in tropical habitats." Moreover the Africans were skilled in metalwork, smelting, blacksmithing, toolmaking, woodworking, weaving, pottery production, rope making, leatherwork, brick making, thatching, and other crafts.[331] Africans were also more desirable as slaves because they were immune to Old World diseases, which caused Native Americans to sicken and die, and, most important, Africans had nowhere to run, unlike the Native Americans, who could escape from slavery into their own familiar territory. Although the Irish were also in an alien land, they were perceived as unruly and violent. When they escaped, they often joined their fellow Catholics, the Spanish and the French, in conspiracies against the English.[332]

Thus, Africans became the preferred slaves because they had the knowledge and skills that made it possible to put them to work immediately to develop the colonies and not because of their physical differences. But the physical differences became the dominant factor as those who profited from their labor needed to justify their inhumanity. According to historian Philip D. Morgan, "The only

331 Id.

332 Id.

effective way to justify slavery was to exclude its victims from the community of man."[333]

The need to protect the institution of slavery in America grew as profits from slavery grew and wealth built on the backs of slaves escalated. While the exact numbers or percentages of slave owners may not be calculated, it is safe to say that the institution of slavery conferred beneficial status to whites at the cost to the African for generations.[334]

In June 2000, Craig Venter, a pioneer of DNA sequencing, observed, "The concept of race has no genetic or scientific basis."[335]

> "...genetic research has revealed two deep truths about people. The first is that all humans are closely related—more closely related than all chimps, even though there are many more humans around today. Everyone has the same collection of genes, but with the exception of identical twins, everyone has slightly different versions of some of them. Studies of this genetic diversity have allowed scientists to reconstruct a kind of family tree of human populations that has revealed the second deep truth: In a very real sense, all people alive today are Africans."[336]

In other words, the conception of race is a social ideation designed to justify disparate treatment between people, without any basis in science.

Lie 3: Genetics, not environment is the driving force of our differences

Americans regularly justified its mistreatment of African Americans based on the lie that blacks were intellectually inferior by virtue of their genetics. For years, scientists sought to prove that there was a divinely determined intellectual hierarchy among people based on the fallacy of race. Defenders of slavery in America relied on what became known as scientific racism.[337]

---

333 Id.

334 Did Only 1.4 Percent of White Americans Own Slaves in 1860? retrieved from https://www.snopes.com/news/2019/08/07/percent-of-whites-owned-slaves/

335 Elizabeth Kolbert, There's No Scientific Basis For Race—It's a Made Up Label, National Geographic, March 12, 2018 retrieved from https://www.nationalgeographic.com/magazine/2018/04/race-genetics-science-africa/

336 Id.

337 Id.

The truth is that intellectual superiority and inferiority based on race is a lie designed and repeated to keep white supremacy alive. The fact that it is a lie is not well hidden. In fact, the 1911 Encyclopedia indirectly acknowledges the truth in its descriptive discussion of the Negro.

> "Mentally the negro is inferior to the white: The remark of F. Manetta, made after a long study of the negro in America, may be taken as generally true of the whole race: "the negro children were sharp, intelligent and full of vivacity, but on approaching the adult period a gradual change set in. The intellect seemed to become clouded, animation giving place to a sort of lethargy, briskness yielding to indolence. We must necessarily suppose that the development of the negro and white proceeds on different lines. While with the latter the volume of the brain grows with the expansion of the brainpan, in the former the growth of the brain is on the contrary arrested by the premature closing of the cranial sutures and lateral pressure of the frontal bone.... This explanation is reasonable and even probable as a contributing cause; but evidence is lacking on the subject and the arrest or even deterioration in mental development is no doubt very largely due to the fact that after puberty sexual matters take the first place in the negro's life and thoughts."[338]

The source continues:

> "though the mental inferiority of the negro to the white or yellow races is a fact, it has often been exaggerated; the negro is largely the creature of his environment, and it is not fair to judge of his mental capacity by tests taken directly from the environment of the white man, as for instance tests in mental arithmetic; skill in reckoning is necessary to the white race, and it has cultivated this faculty; but it is not necessary to the negro."[339]

These and other lies like them that result in the denial of truth served to create an alternative reality firmly embraced by whites in their unyielding effort to retain their ill-gotten status. If we are to move forward as a nation and world,

---

338 Thomas Athol Joyce and Walter Francis Willcox, Negro, 1911 Encyclopedia Britannica, Vol 19, 11th Ed. Pp344-349 Cambridge, England at the University Press, retrieved from https://babel.hathitrust.org/cgi/pt?id=nnc1.cu06905960&view=1up&seq=372&q1=negro

339 Id.

we must not keep falling for these lies of inhumanity and accept the truth that we are all people with the traits, habits, intelligence and frailties of all human beings. After centuries of deviling people because of their race[340], nationalities, religion, all proven baseless, we must move forward into the future of humanity.

340 E.g. see supra n. 334, Kolbert, reporting the scientific racist view that white people are innately superior to all other races, with yellow people coming in at second; and see the history of English deviling Irish as savages; and see David Livingstone, Less than Human: The Psychology of Cruelty, NPR, March 29, 2011, retrieved from https://www.npr.org/2011/03/29/134956180/criminals-see-their-victims-as-less-than-human discussing for example, the grotesquely inhumane belief that Jews are

CHAPTER 8

Ensuring that all communities are communities of opportunity

"However much it is denied, however many excuses are made, the hard cold fact is that many white Americans oppose open housing because they unconsciously, and often consciously, feel that the Negro is innately inferior, impure, depraved and degenerate,"[341]

Martin Luther King, Jr.

THE COLD WITHIN
By James Patrick Kinney

Six humans trapped by happenstance
In dark and bitter cold
Each one possessed a stick of wood,
Or so the story's told.

Their dying fire in need of logs,
The first woman held hers back.
For on the faces around the fire,
She noticed one was black.

The next man looking cross the way,
Saw one not of his church,
And couldn't bring himself to give
The fire his stick of birch.

341 Martin Luther King, Jr., *Where do we go from here: Chaos or Community*, 1967. Beacon Press

The third one sat in tattered clothes,
He gave his coat a hitch.
Why should his log be put to use,
To warm the idle rich?

The rich man just sat back and thought
Of the wealth he had in store.
And how to keep what he had earned
From the lazy, shiftless poor.

The black man's face bespoke revenge
As the fire passed from sight,
For all he saw in his stick of wood
Was a chance to spite the white.

The last man of this forlorn group
Did naught except for gain
Giving only to those who gave
Was how he played the game.

The logs held tight in death's still hands
Was proof of human sin.
They didn't die from the cold without,
They died from ---THE COLD WITHIN.

COMMUNITY UNIFICATION

America is not unique in its enslavement of people or even in the savagery that accompanied the barbaric practice of slavery.[342] Early evidence of the institution is reflected in the Babylonian Code of Hammurabi in the 18th century BC, seventh century BC in Greece, and second century BC in Rome.[343] The slave class

342 History of Slavery, retrieved from http://www.historyworld.net/wrldhis/PlainTextHistories.asp?historyid=ac41 The Cambridge World History of Slavery: The Ancient Mediterranean, Cambridge University Press, retrieved from http://assets.cambridge.org/97805218/40668/frontmatter/9780521840668_frontmatter.pdf

343 Id.

was generally viewed as different from the slaveholder class by religion, language, birthplace, and physical characteristics.[344] Through the centuries slaves were of all races and ethnicities.

During the Middle Ages most slaves serving in western Europe were of "Slavic" origins from central and eastern Europe. In Germany during the tenth century, the word sclavus had become synonymous with slave. In Europe, Italian merchants continued to buy large numbers of Slavic prisoners along the Dalmatian coast. During the thirteenth century, western Europeans began to intercept people under foreign rule—from Caucasia to the eastern Balkans—to force them into slavery. These captives were Armenians, Circassians, Georgians, Abkhazians, Mingrelians, Russians, Tartars, Albanians, and Bulgarians—a very multicultural group. These "slavs" were exported to Mediterranean markets; mainly Egypt, Syria, Cyprus, and Sicily, where local traders were willing to pay a good price for their services. [345]

Whatever the culture, the slaveholder considered themselves superior to the slave. This superiority characteristic became inextricably tied to race in the United States. The nation's laws, policies, social structure, scientific perspectives, and judicial rulings were overwhelmingly structured to deny rights and access to African Americans in order to shore up perceptions of white supremacy. The necessity for supremacy is foundational to American life, and its roots permeate the regressive and progressive concepts of life for Americans of color. Its vestiges transcend ethnicities, races, and cultures. It is certainly the basis for the historical legacy of housing discrimination in this country, and also the failures of so many curative efforts, including the Fair Housing Act. There are specific strategies that must be taken if these constructions are to be eliminated.

CHOOSING COMMUNITY OVER CHAOS

Change, while inevitable, is often difficult to accept. When it comes to how Americans perceive one another, we must be willing to consider our fundamental likenesses. As Americans, we have numerous ideals that we value, including

344 Paul E. Lovejoy, Mariana P. Candido and Yacine Daddi Addoun, Slavery and Race, updated Apr 29, 2020, Encyclopedia.com retrieved from https://www.encyclopedia.com/social-sciences/encyclopedias-almanacs-transcripts-and-maps/slavery-and-race

345 Id. Lovejoy

freedom, liberty, free press, religious choice and practice, wealth, power, privacy, guns, individualism, and that out of many comes one (*e pluribus unum*). Americans tend to believe in equality, justice, fair play. But lying beneath these fundamental shared beliefs, Americans developed and have retained stereotypical perceptions of citizens who do not share the same race, gender, religion. We have collective perceptions that describe Americans by race, gender, religion, and even where we live in the country.

National perceptions like "white is right and Black get back," and misogynistic ideals rooted in patriarchy where such sayings akin to "a women's place is in the kitchen," have undergirded policies effortlessly and with such an overbearing power, that we often don't view the problem(s) as ours. We view it as "theirs," and we, the humane, the compassionate, the benevolent are here to solve "their" problems.

We seek to do for ourselves by ourselves even as we surely must recognize that there are and will be times when we need the collective help of our friends and neighbors. We subsidize each other, wealthy and poor alike. From the corporate bailouts during the panic of 1792 and again in 1893, Pres. Franklin D. Roosevelt's New Deal bail-out that put Americans back to work in the 1930s and 40s, to the Marshall Plan's bailout of Europe, to the COVID bail-out, and all the bailouts in between, Americans have a long history of reaching down and reaching out to give a hand up. In less than one month after the United States recognized the Covid-19 pandemic, wealthy corporations sought help from the federal government and found it in the hands of the taxpayers—it took corporations less than a month to ask for a lifeline.[346] At the same time, we realized that lower- and middle income families also needed assistance; so we, the taxpayers, collectively provided resources because of a cultural belief that as Americans, we are called on to help our neighbors.

Our nation's historical policies of racial segregation, neglect of impoverished people, and economic laissez-faire have resulted in massive disparities in housing based on race and wealth. Relishing in the suffering of others, let alone causing it, is not part of our shared American culture. We have been slowly emerging from an assembly of laws based in large part on political and social policies that favored racial segregation and denied housing and land ownership. But we have done so based on explicit and implicit biases that suggest that some Americans

346 CBS NEWS. Airlines seek $50 billion U.S. bailout to survive coronavirus turbulence. 16 Mar 2020. retrieved at https://www.cbsnews.com/news/airlines-seek-50-billion-bailout-from-u-s-to-survive-coronavirus-turbulence/

are better or more deserving than others because of their race, gender, or ethnicity. This false narrative will surely cause us to linger in chaos if we fail to take affirmative actions toward viable and sustainable solutions.

I call this concept of solution-baiting, community unification.

UNIFYING THE COMMUNITY: IT'S TEAMWORK

"The strength of the team is each individual member. The strength of each member is the team."

- Phil Jackson[347]

"He who masters the power formed by a group of people working together has within his grasp one of the greatest powers [ever] known."

- Idowu Koyenikan[348]

One of the characteristics of a civil society is that the members show respect to fellow citizens and people believe that other members are worthy of respect.[349] The Universal Declaration of Human Rights was adopted by the United Nations General Assembly in Paris in 1948.[350] Its goal was to grant status worthy of respect to all human beings everywhere. No human being is exempt.

When we respect others, it affirms a right to respect and their worthiness of respect. On the other hand, when we withhold respect from others, we imply they are unworthy of it. This can trigger a decline that is exceedingly difficult to arrest and end. Once it is generally believed that a certain race or ethnic group or nationality or skin color or gender or age is unworthy of respect, the flood gates open for abuse, prejudice, and harassment.[351] These beliefs and the

---

347 American basketball player and coach of the NBA champions Chicago Bulls and LA Lakers.

348 Idowu Koyenikan, All you need is a Ball: What Soccer Teaches us about Success in Life and Business,

349 Samuel Rodenhizer, Why respect is Important in Life, A Conscious Rethink retrieved from https://www.aconsciousrethink.com/8558/respecting-others/

350 The United Nations General Assembly in Paris, The Universal Declaration of Human Rights, General Assembly resolution 217A, December 10, 1948 which also included in its Article 13 the right to freedom of movement and residence within the borders of each state

351 Rodenhizer, supra n. 348.

resulting behaviors have been routinely displayed in the past two centuries in particular. The natural and logical outcome of the removal of respect from particular classes is first rejection, then discrimination, then abuse, and ultimately genocide.

The father of modern psychiatry, William James said, "The deepest principle in human nature is the craving to be appreciated." Those who are not appreciated do not feel respected. It's disheartening.

The history of the struggle for civil rights throughout the world is the struggle to win respect from others. The American Founding Fathers expressed it in the United States Declaration of Independence this way:

> *"We hold these truths to be self-evident, that all men are created equal, that they are endowed by their Creator with certain unalienable rights that among these are Life, Liberty, and the pursuit of Happiness."*

Respect for human beings entails the granting, preserving, and protection of these rights. Without respect, these rights will be missing. And if these rights are missing, respect will be missing too. They exist together.

"Throughout history, the human experience has been extremely brutal".[352] Our historical experiences show that as human beings we have fed people to the lions, beheaded them, burned them alive, tarred and feathered them, lynched them, crucified them, electrocuted them in chairs, and subjected them to indescribable torture. Despite unspeakable and horrible atrocities in our current era, we may actually be becoming more civilized." As reassuring as it may be that we are kinder to each other now than we once were, it would seem that some further evolution is needed in order for us to appreciate and care for each other on a regular basis.

So, what is the continuing cause of our disrespect for one another? What is it that creates so much isolation, loneliness, and separation, to reimage others who appear different from us as the enemy? Why do we treat each other with such disregard and dislike? Is it because we project our hidden fears onto others,

352 Ed and Seb Shapiro, The Blog, Why Do We Treat each other with Such Disregard and Disrespect?, citingAndrew Cohen retrieved from https://www.huffpost.com/entry/why-do-we-treat-each-othe_b_795508

making them the problem that needs to be annihilated, rather than seeing that a phobia and intolerance actually lie within ourselves?[353]

Wealth warrants respect

Americans value wealth and devalue poverty. Those who are wealthy are respected because they have affluence. Those who lack wealth are disrespected because they are poor. The gap between rich and poor continues to expand and the specific wealth gap between white Americans and African Americans is massive.[354] In fact, African Americans have less than ten percent of white wealth.[355] This racial wealth gap exists even among Blacks who are highly educated and come from two-parent homes. Black families with graduate or professional degrees have $200,000 less in wealth than similarly-educated whites. Even more jarring, white high school dropouts are wealthier than Black and Latino college graduates. Similarly, two-parent Black households have less wealth than single-parent white households. This sustained and growing disparity did not occur by happenstance, but as the result of continuous racially prejudiced policies and practices. For example, state benefits like the Transitional Assistance for Needy Families and the Supplemental Nutrition Assistance Program, forbid beneficiaries from accumulating wealth. In some states, recipients of these state benefits were not allowed to save more than $1,000 or to own cars worth more than $4,650.24.[356] These anti-wealth policies directly conflict with the national policies that promote wealth building.

---

353 Id.

354 William Darity Jr., Darrick Hamilton, Mark Paul, Alan Aja, Anne Price, Antonio Moore, and Caterina Chiopris, What we get Wrong about Closing the Racial Wealth Gap, Samuel DuBois Cook Center on Social Equity, April 2018 accessed at https://socialequity.duke.edu/wp-content/uploads/2020/01/what-we-get-wrong.pdf

355 U.S. Census Bureau. "Wealth, Asset Ownership, & Debt of Households Detailed Tables: 2016," Download "Wealth and Asset Ownership for Households, by Type of Asset and Selected Characteristics: 2016 retrieved from https://www.census.gov/data/tables/2016/demo/wealth/wealth-asset-ownership.html.

356 Kimberly Amadeo, racial Wealth Gap in the United States, Is there a way to close it and fill the divide? April 2020, retrieved from https://www.thebalance.com/racial-wealth-gap-in-united-states-4169678#citation-2 citing Georgia Department of Human Services. "TANF Eligibility Requirements." retrieved from https://dfcs.georgia.gov/tanf-eligibility-requirements and Washington State Department of Health and Human Services. "How Vehicles Count Toward the Resource Limit for Cash and Food." retrieved from https://www.dshs.wa.gov/esa/resources/how-vehicles-count-toward-resource-limit-cash-and-food

> "Each year, the federal government offers around $400 billion in tax cuts designed to build wealth, according to the Corporation for Enterprise Development. At least 34% of the cuts promote homeownership, while another third subsidizes savings and investment. A 2018 Duke University study *reported that reducing the* racial homeownership gap would narrow the racial wealth gap by 31%. The cuts help the wealthy more than the poor. The wealthiest 5% of Americans are in the best financial position to take advantage of these tax cuts. As a result, half of the $400 billion goes to them. The middle 60% only receive 4% of these tax cuts. The bottom 20% of taxpayers get almost nothing."[357]

Without dramatic changes to policies in education, finance, homeownership, housing, and our own perceptions about the problems of racial disparity in our country, it is inane to expect different outcomes. The facts show that despite the many personal efforts that African Americans make, higher education attainment, buying homes, and working, their incomes and wealth still are well below their white peers. The systemic gaps will not be closed merely from making a greater effort.

DESTROYING THE MYTHOLOGICAL BOOTSTRAP

One of the crippling myths underlying the digression of many of our country's people is that they have somehow been hoisted by their own petards and that their resulting despair is of their own making and can be fixed or cured by their own efforts and diligence. The psychological concept known as the "fundamental attribution error" addresses this tendency to see the behavior of others as being determined by their character – while excusing our own behavior based on circumstances. The belief that one can make it on their own but, would instead choose to languish in poverty is rooted in idiocy that supports disrespect. The myth substantiates a basis for one person's disrespect of the other and often decries one's disrespect for herself. Over long periods of time, the myth is launched at entire groups of people—racial, ethnicity, gender—and any act of the group is viewed as unworthy. Unworthy of our respect, and altogether

357 Kimberly Amadeo, racial Wealth Gap in the United States, Is there a way to close it and fill the divide?, April 2020, retrieved from https://www.thebalance.com/racial-wealth-gap-in-united-states-4169678#citation-2

unworthy of our concern. Unworthy of our concern, no corrective action need be taken.

EFFECTS OF DISRESPECT

Racially based or racially informed disregard (or ill will) is an indifference (or opposition) to another's welfare on account of the racial group to which she is assigned.[358] The health effects of racism are well documented. A group of Harvard researchers found that a mere 1% increase in incidences of racial disrespect translates to an increase in 350 deaths per 100,000 African Americans. Being on the receiving of overt or subtle racism creates intense and constant stress which boosts the risk of depression, anxiety and anger—factors that can lead to or aggravate heart disease. Some research suggests racism can also manifest itself in respiratory and other physical problems.[359]

Racism also has psychological implications for the racist. Dr. Carl Bell, MD,[360] described these individuals having a psychopathological defect/narcissistic personality disorder which allows for dehumanization of others. Other psychiatrists have opined that racism may meet the criteria for a full psychotic disorder and Dr. Alvin Poussaint, MD,[361] explains that "extreme racism" is a type of delusional disorder.

The cost of racism is also exhibited by recognizing that racism, as one of the root causes of poverty, costs our nation huge amounts of money, measured in crime, unemployment, and related social ills.[362] Racism, practiced as housing discrimination, also creates white ghettoes, impacting white children and adults who are isolated from interacting with diverse cultures and people.[363] As long as we devalue diverse communities and cultures then it is easier to understand why

---

358 Joshua Glasgow. Racism as Disrespect. Ethics, Vol. 120, No. 1 (October 2009), pp. 64-93; 67

359 See Sid Kirchheimer, Racism is Harmful to Health, Antiracism Initiatives Needed, but Slow to be recognized, say Experts, accessed at https://www.webmd.com/mental-health/news/20030109/racism-is-harmful-to-health#1

360 Bell CC. Racism, narcissism, and integrity. J Natl Med Assoc. 1978;70:89-92.

361 Poussaint AF. Is extreme racism a mental illness? West J Med. 2002;176:4.

362 Horace Seldon, Convictions About Racism in the United States of America, Racism: Negative Effects on Whites, November, 1991 accessed at http://horaceseldon.com/racism-negative-effects-on-whites/

363 Id.

we fail to meet the goals of the Fair Housing Act. When we view policy through a white lens, we embrace the myth of white superiority and continue to act in ways that disparage African American communities.

The impact of such underlying racism expressed as implicit bias is apparent from many of the pro-housing advocacy discussions in cases like *Inclusive Communities.* It is uncontested that America's cities remain separated by race. Housing advocates believe that governmental acts that locate public and other low-income housing in areas where the population is densely Black do not "affirmatively further" fair housing under the Act. One of the sponsors of the Act, Senator Edward Brooke believed that the Act would "unlock the door [to the black ghettoes] for those who are able and choose to leave." Almost fifty years later, in a 2007 opinion, Chief Justice Roberts wrote that, "the way to stop discrimination on the basis of race is to stop discriminating on the basis of race."[364]

Housing integration has always been a touchy subject made even more controversial when advocates rely on data that moving African Americans from their own communities to so-called "high-opportunity" areas produces better outcomes for them and their future than for the African American residents who were left behind. Yet, the comparison is anything but comparable. One should expect that people in communities with maintained infrastructure, supermarkets, financial institutions, businesses, access to transportation, good education, and other amenities that ensure strong communities would fare better than living in communities that fail to offer those benefits. At least one recent study suggests that even if African Americans live in advantaged neighborhoods they may not reap or experience similar benefits compared to white counterparts in those same communities due to systemic undervaluation of the race.[365]

Research has also shown that a child's neighborhood effects how they fare academically, economically, and physically; it also predicts how they interact with the criminal justice system. Neighborhoods do matter; but the central

364 Parents Involved in Community Schools v Seattle School Dist. No. 1 et.al. No. 05–908. Argued December 4, 2006—Decided June 28, 2007

365 Junia Howell, The Truly Advantaged: Examining the Effects of Privileged Places on Educational Attainment, The Sociological Quarterly, 60:3, 420-438, DOI: 10.1080/00380253.2019.1580546 The Sociological Quarterly, 60:3, 420-438, DOI: 10.1080/00380253.2019.1580546 The Sociological Quarterly, 60:3, 420-438, DOI: 10.1080/00380253.2019.1580546 opining that "Generational advantages (legacy admissions, family wealth), social networks that give white kids preference in private school and college admissions, and institutional practices (like inequality in high school "tracking") may all play a role."

assumption that poor areas—and the people who live in them—are the problem fails. To solve these centuries-long racial disparities, we must look not only at the places, but also the institutions both inside and outside those communities.[366]

Our current paradigm views white communities as innately better. We look for ways for black people to escape the hell of their own neighborhoods to reach the heavenly white community ones. Instead, we must respectfully recognize the obligation to ensure that all communities can fairly provide opportunities to its residents. In other words, rather than acting on the basis that white communities deserve to have better and are fundamentally better because of their whiteness; act from the posture that all communities deserve to be of a quality that provides opportunities for its residents.

Viewed through the inclusion lens, needed infrastructure, repair and rebuilding of long abandoned communities so that they will be attractive to various income residents. Communities across a city would benefit from these investment dollars. Instead of only mostly or entirely white neighborhoods providing opportunities, historically marginalized neighborhoods would benefit from investments in their community so that they too could provide opportunity. This all-communities approach decries the notion that blacks can only prosper if they are in white communities and destroys the justification for restricting investment to green-lined white communities. While this "all communities" posture is based on equality, it cannot be viewed as an end-all. It must be part of transformational change to be effective. Some strategies that affect this progression include progressive taxation, child savings accounts limited to education and homeownership, and income equality.[367]

Whites move into predominantly African American communities for multiple reasons, but on moving in, immediately demand that long neglected facilities and infrastructures are enhanced—transforming a systemically neglected community to one of opportunity. The transformation is not based on race, although our historical policies certainly will not eliminate race from the equation, but instead is based on the injection of services and resources in and to the area. Taking federal housing dollars from poor neighborhoods to build affordable housing in nicer neighborhoods ensures that poorer areas will continue to

366 Id.

367 Kimberly Amadeo, supra n. 356 https://www.thebalance.com/racial-wealth-gap-in-united-states-4169678#

struggle even more.[368] Instead, change must include robust investment of public dollars in African American and other long-neglected minority neighborhoods.

Communities of Opportunity should not be reduced to an either-or proposition; either move from devalued Black communities to white communities of opportunity or languish in the deteriorating communities of color. Instead the goal must be that all communities, whether racially identifiable or not, would be communities of opportunity.

368 Alana Semuels, Has America Given up on the Dream of Racial Integration?, The Atlantic, June 19, 2015, accessed at https://www.theatlantic.com/business/archive/2015/06/segregation-2015/396167/

CHAPTER 9
Respect Is Not Enough

Wealth that has been handed down from generation to generation is often referred to as "old money", while first generation wealth is considered "new money". As we humans seem to do, we distinguish the old money aristocracy from the new money upstarts. The aristocracy deserves to be rich...it is their birthright while the new money is often considered "rags-to-riches" or self-made wealthy. However the wealthy distinguish themselves, for the rest of us, money and wealth are the most dynamic bases for achievement. The underside of that simple analysis is that really new money, say lotto winners' money seems to portend a different destiny. Lottery winners are more likely to declare bankruptcy within three to five years than the average American.[369] It seems logical that people who start something altogether new will take time to learn how to master the new task. That is, for people who have never had money, it may take time to learn what to do to grow it rather than lose it. Respect is important and wealth has a way of garnering respect. But respect without wealth won't make up for centuries of intentional policies and laws designed to ensure that people of color, but especially African Americans, would be denied basic human rights, constitutional rights, and opportunity to excel. Respect without wealth won't bridge the racial gaps and disproportionalities that exist in America.

---

369 Abigail Johnson Hess, Here's why lottery winners go broke, CNBC August 2017 retrieved from https://www.cnbc.com/2017/08/25/heres-why-lottery-winners-go-broke.html

American jurisprudence has long recognized the right of the injured to recover damages from the offender.[370] There is also a common legal tenet that those who have benefited from ill-gotten gains will be required to purge themselves of such gains.[371] There should be no question that the United States government and private industries caused significant injuries to African American citizens across every political, social and legal spectrum over the past 300 plus years.[372] But even with that knowledge, questions remain regarding how African Americans can be made whole? How do you quantify the damages and how should such damages be paid?

Americans generally expect offenders to be remorseful and to show their remorse and atone for it.[373] Transforming culture so that people can relate to each other from a point of equality than one of superiority/inferiority exhibits the remorse, but it is insufficient to remedy the wrong. One effort made to quantify the damages suffered comes in between 18.6 trillion USD to 6.2 quadrillion USD.[374] These numbers may be low as further research is required to estimate the cost of lost opportunities (LC) and pain and suffering (PS). Further research

370 Robert M. Lloyd & Nicholas J. Chase, Recovery Of Damages For Lost Profits:

The Historical Development, Uni of Penn Journal Business and Law Vol 18:2, retrieved at https://scholarship.law.upenn.edu/cgi/viewcontent.cgi?article=1507&context=jbl

371 Brent Kendall, Supreme Court Case Tests FTC's Powers to Recoup Ill-Gotten Gains, Wall Street Journal, Jan 21, 2021. retrieved at https://www.wsj.com/articles/supreme-court-case-tests-ftcs-powers-to-recoup-ill-gotten-gains-11610572799

372 Richard Rothstein, The Color of Law, ISBN 978-1-63149-453-6, Liveright Publ.Co.2017

373 See generally, Mary Louise Kelly, Host npr news, Capitol Rioter who Walked on Senate Floor on January 6 sentenced to 8 months in prison, July 19, 2021 retrieved from M. Eve Hanan, Remorse Bias, 83 Mo.L.Rev. 301 (Spring 2018) https://www.npr.org/transcripts/1017916061 reporting that the defendant "said he was truly remorseful and regretful for what he did on January 6. He said, quote, "I say this not because I face consequence, but because of the damage that day's incident caused, the way this country that I love has been hurt. He said it was a, quote, "foolish decision" and that he takes full responsibility for it." And see Alayna Jehle, Monica K. Miller and Markus Kemmelmeier, The Influence of Accounts and Remorse on Mock Jurors' Judgments of Offenders, 33 Law & Hum. Beh. 393, 394-396 October 2009 discussing the impact of a defendant's remorse and finding that expressions of remorse were often followed by reduced sentences or lighter punishments

374 Thomas Craemer, Trevor Smith, Brianna Harrison, Trevon Logan, Wesley Bellamy and William Darity, Jr., Wealth Implications of Slavery and Racial Discrimination for African American Descendants of the Enslaved, Vol. 47 The Review of Black Political Economy, Issue 3, pp 218-254 June 2020, ISSN 0034-6446, Digital Object Identifier 10.1177/0034644620926516, retrieved from https://www.researchgate.net/publication/342315758_Wealth_Implications_of_Slavery_and_Racial_Discrimination_for_African_American_Descendants_of_the_Enslaved/link/5f1ae98592851cd5fa42364c/download

is also required to estimate the costs of colonial slavery, as well as racial discrimination following the abolition of slavery in the United States to African American descendants of the enslaved.[375]

Failure to adequately compensate the injured will not fill the huge gaps the injuries caused, instead the injured parties will be required to jump over these cavernous chasms with few, if any, resources to effectively bridge the gap, thus dooming most to a perennial underclass status.

Like cultural transformation, compensation for people wronged will not be easy. Respect centers our moral obligations to value each other as human beings. But ultimately it is wealth that allows equivalency between the classes. America's wealth gap began with the arrival of the European settlers. Ever since these settlers took over properties owned and inhabited by Native Americans and redistributed the lands through land grants reserved only to white men, the wealth gap in America emerged and has since then been nurtured. From that time to this, and particularly after 1979, the wealth gap has exploded, with U.S. incomes polarized between the top income earning 1% and the bottom 99%. Upon closer inspection, according to some research, if the 99% group was further divided, those in the 90th-99th percentile own most of the wealth.[376] Moreover, "had the more equitable income distributions of the three decades following World War II (1945 through 1974) merely held steady, the aggregate annual income of Americans earning below the 90th percentile would have been $2.5 trillion higher in the year 2018 alone. That is an amount equal to nearly 12 percent of GDP—enough to more than double median income—enough to pay every single working American in the bottom nine deciles an additional $1,144 a month. Every month. Every single year."[377]

This illustrates the extent to which government policies have contributed to the wealth gap generally, and to the race wealth gap specifically. To cure these disparities, the offenders that include the government as well as identifiable

375 Id.

376 Professor Michael Lind, The Myth of the 99%, the bellows, November 25, 2020 where the professor provides the following example: "the top 1 percent owns 56 percent. The bottom 99 percent own only 44 percent of stocks. This seems to support the 99 Percent Theory. ...The 99 percent are divided into two groups. The bottom 90 percent own only 12 percent of stocks owned by households. The rest of the stock—32 percent—is owned by those in the 90th-99th percentile, made up overwhelmingly by college-educated members of the overclass." The remaining stock 56% is owned by the 1% retrieved from https://www.thebellows.org/the-myth-of-the-99/

377 Carter C. Price, Kathryn A. Edwards, Trends in Income from 1975 to 2018, Santa Monica, CA: RAND Corporation, 2020. https://www.rand.org/pubs/working_papers/WRA516-1.html.

private beneficiaries must pay through the enactment of sustainable policies to right the wrongs and by funding the people who have borne the burden of these disparities for so long.

Reparations include everything necessary to make amends for the wrong. As such reparations includes but is not limited to money.

There is some evidence that the government has begun work on bridging historical wealth inequities through legislation like those addressed in executive orders signed by the President that among other things:

- Directed the attorney general not to renew contracts between the Department of Justice (but not other federal agencies) and privately operated criminal detention centers. Private prisons operate to make a profit which relies on filling the prisons with people, who have historically been African Americans and other minorities. These private prisons are reminiscent of the post emancipation convict leasing systems adopted in former slave states to ensure that former slaves retained their slavery status of working for free. Mostly African American males but African American females, as well, would be picked up by police and charged with crimeless crimes to justify the enslavement in local jails and prison, so that they would perform slave labor for private companies and individuals.[378]

- In a presidential memorandum, directing the Department of Housing and Urban Develop to examine the prior administration's actions that undermined fair housing policies and laws. The department is also directed to take steps to fully implement the requirements of the Fair Housing Act. Of course, as pointed out by this author, the Act needs to be interpreted through lens of inclusion and not lens of white superiority

- An executive order that federal agencies regularly and meaningfully engage with Tribal governments.

---

378 See Michelle Alexander, The New Jim Crow: Mass Incarceration in the Age of Colorblindness, The New Press, Jan 7, 2020; and see Michael Hardy, Blood and Sugar, Texas Monthly Magazine, retrieved from https://www.texasmonthly.com/articles/sugar-land-slave-convict-labor-history/

- In a presidential memorandum, directed the Department of Health and Human Services to advance health equity and to consider advancing "cultural competency" and sensitivity toward Asian Americans and Pacific Islanders.

- COVID related initiatives that include massive economic stimuli, that includes a $15 federal minimum wage.

- Investing billions of dollars for community revitalization in African American communities for infrastructure improvements, transportation and business development.

Efforts like these can be positive moves toward equality, but we have allowed the equality gap to get so large across every platform that no one administration, no one corporation, no single person will be able to get it done. It must be collective in developing meaningful solutions and collective in implementation. It must

- take into account diverse perspectives through inclusion of socially, economically and politically different people,

- provide transformative solutions that establishes a wide, deep, and independent foundation in wealth among black Americans that include reparations

- effectively address disparities in debt, education, wages, housing stability, business prosperity,[379]

- reject the false narrative that African Americans are alone to blame for their status and

- acknowledge and address the fundamental truth that the very root of America's failure in fulfilling its promise of equality is

---

379 Suzanne Kahn, Mark Huelsman and Jen Mishory, Bridging Progressive Policy Debates: How Student Debt and the Racial Wealth Gap Reinforce Each Other, retrieved from https://vtechworks.lib.vt.edu/bitstream/handle/10919/97813/StudentDebt20190.pdf?sequence=1

> its racialized laws, policies and practices that rest on the false foundation of white supremacy.[380]

It should be a national imperative to dismantle these disparities and false narratives and to provide equal opportunity for all Americans.

380 See for e.g. William Darity, Jr., Darrick Hamilton, Mark Paul, Alan Aja, Anne Price, Antonio Moore and Caterina Chiopris, What We get Wrong about Closing the Racial Wealth Gap, 2018, retrieved from http://narrowthegap.org/images/documents/Wealth-Gap---FINAL-COMPLETE-REPORT.pdf

Epilogue

Human beings have distinctive characteristics. We can show compassion for others, we can be honest, courageous, responsible, kind, creative and forward-thinking. We can be self-aware and we can think for ourselves. On the other hand, Albert Einstein warned that the "mediocre mind is incapable of understanding the man who refuses to bow blindly to conventional prejudices and chooses instead to express his opinions courageously and honestly." Much of what has guided us, as humans through the centuries, is based on conventional prejudices and habitual thinking. The shape of our world, gender roles, stereotyping, economic systems, culture, public policy, societal norms have all been based on conventional prejudices. It's often easier to accept the current condition without supporting change or evolution even if it is to evolve to a better human being. But our ability to question and to think critically for ourselves is what will direct us to see the world and our places in it differently.

For much of our history, we have created false bases for superiority; birthright, gender, religion, geography, and race to name a few. American history is fraught with examples of all types and levels of superiority; with one of the most damning being racial superiority. It lies on a bed of pretense and pretext and is so easily refutable its sustainability is curious. Throughout this book, I have shown how the embrace of white superiority has resulted in grotesquely inhumane policies and actions that have fueled ever widening racial disparities and disproportionalities.

The notion of superiority has fed some of our most sustained conventions that identify who are more entitled, more valuable, less persecuted and less prosecuted. It has also required us to dehumanize people in order to justify overabundance for some while relegating others to suffer under gross inequities. With white superiority, for example, the Supreme Court furthered whites' justifications for their bounty by declaring that blacks were not human even as their own actions and deeds showed that the justices clearly recognized it as a lie. White men may have liaised with non- humans but such liaisons did not produce their children. The point being that dehumanization is merely a tool used to justify the horrors that supremacy shields.

And upon this lie of white supremacy an empire rose and if we fail to collectively change, reform, transform our systems, it is on the back of white supremacy that the empire will fall.

Superiority needs no handicap, no special policy to manifest. By its very nature the superior will dominate without special advantage. That inherency reveals the fallacy of white supremacy. Far from inherency, whites have had to create and guard every possible advantage that gave them preference over others, especially the African American. These exclusive advantages occur in housing as shown in this book, but also in education, employment, business, judiciary, health, social, sports, art, science, medicine, and all others. These exclusive advantages are designed to ensure that the field will never be level but shall be bent in their favor. Such advantages are not needed by the truly superior because their dominance would be imminent. Even in the struggle for equity, these supremacists staunchly resist actually leveling the field. In fact, they would do anything...including destroying democracy itself, to ensure that the field remained indecently uneven.

The scandal extends far beyond the fallacy of white supremacy, we must acknowledge that white Anglo Saxons have dehumanized the Indigenous Americans, Irish Americans, Jewish Americans, Mexican Americans and people of color generally. History also reveals that regardless of race or color, male supremacy misconceptions continue to support policies and practices that relegate women to an inferior status. Humans appear to have an insatiable desire for hatred which spotlights the depth of the fear of equality but fails to explain why a people who purportedly pride themselves in ensuring equality would work so feverishly to deny and destroy it.[381] The existence and threat of supremacy must be eliminated.

381 See generally Zwiers, M, 'Aryans and Anglo-Saxons: Segregationist Visions of the Postwar World', Paper presented at Forging the American Century, Nijmegen, Netherlands, 10.27-28.2016 (abstract)

www.ingramcontent.com/pod-product-compliance
Lightning Source LLC
LaVergne TN
LVHW022102200926
848481LV00003B/1046